Beyond the Consent of the Governed

Ronald Reagan, George W. Bush, Barack Obama, and the Erosion of American Values

CRAIG M. FARNHAM

Copyright © 2016 Craig M. Farnham
All rights reserved
First Edition

PAGE PUBLISHING, INC.
New York, NY

First originally published by Page Publishing, Inc. 2016

ISBN 978-1-68348-873-6 (Paperback)
ISBN 978-1-68348-874-3 (Digital)

Printed in the United States of America

There are several important people to whom I dedicate this book:

Pa

My dad may or may not agree with some of the views as I've expressed them in this book. However, even as I write these words, I feel the rock-solid love he's always shown for his son. In him, I will always have a best friend and a powerful example of how to treat others.

Uncle Russ

In the last few years, I've been very lucky to get to know, respect, and love one of Pa's older siblings: he is a person with whom I share a deep curiosity for art, literature, religion, and politics. His mind is open to the world around him, and his thoughts—shared generously and without guile—push me to continue asking the tough questions.

Scott Lindsay

For as long as I can remember, my older cousin has been more like an older brother whose love and support have never been in short supply. He reminds me often that his door is always open; he does not have to remind me that the same holds true for his heart. Our deep bond is a testament to the fact that family has nothing at all to do with genetics and everything to do with a person's spirit.

Larry Rowlands

My good friend and coworker is a passionate person whose conservatism has, over several years and during countless lunchtime discussions, helped focus my arguments and sharpen my pen. Sometimes we agree, at other times not so much; however, he constantly challenges me to see things from another perspective—and without his help, this book could not have been written.

Kathy Clough

Kathy's political mind has—time and again—been a kind of sharpening stone against which I've been able to focus my efforts. They say one should avoid certain topics (like politics) in polite company; that said, honesty and love of family run much deeper between us than any political contest. While our discussions are riven by geography, I always picture her broad smile as I read her thoughtful, history-infused opinions. And I have to say this: that without her opinions as a guidepost, this book could not have taken shape.

Uncle Frank

My grandma's brother was an amazing person for so many reasons, not the least of which being that he was one of my earliest—and biggest—fans. In a world where kids can be cruel to one another, I had a rough time—it was Uncle Frank who told me that I was special, and to hell with people who couldn't (or wouldn't) take the time to see it. He passed away in 2008, but I know he's still in my corner.

And my grandma,
Jeanne M. Deschamps

Of the many things she gave me, I know I inherited her passion for history and politics. Cancer took her away in 2010, and words can't express how deeply I feel her loss. Her spirit is still with me, though—and always will be—especially in the following pages.

My mother and sister, as well as countless aunts, uncles, cousins, and friends, have made my life more interesting and rewarding than I can begin to describe.

Introduction

My first clear memory of a president of the United States is of an address made from the Oval Office on the evening of January 28, 1986. I was six years old. That morning the nation watched as the space shuttle Challenger lifted off into the sky and, moments after liftoff, exploded. The crew was lost. The president, Ronald Wilson Reagan, had been scheduled to deliver the State of the Union address that evening. The decision was made, however, to make a different sort of address—this one to the American people.

I remember watching the television screen, seeing the kind face sitting behind a large desk. He didn't look like a commanding person, a leader; rather (to my six-year-old mind) he looked like a grandpa. And what he said has stayed with me—and with generations. Speaking of the Challenger crew, Reagan said, "We will never forget them, nor the last time we saw them: this morning, as they waved good-bye and 'slipped the surly bonds of earth' to touch the face of God." I was only six, yet the power of his words hit me even then.

We refer to Ronald Reagan with a kind of nostalgic gloss as the Great Communicator. He was. He had an actor's ability to deliver and—rare in the world of politics—a charm that allowed him to express a compassion that was genuine. His words did not feel empty. During his first inaugural (January 20, 1981), President Reagan said, "It is time to check and reverse the growth of government which shows signs of having grown beyond the consent of the governed." This was the Great Communicator at work, using big, wonderful words. Heartfelt words.

To touch the face of God—these words haunted me the moment he said them.

My second memory of a president is of the same man sitting at the same desk in the Oval Office. On March 4, 1987, he spoke to the same television audience, this time saying, "A few months ago, I told the American people I did not trade arms for hostages. My heart—and my best intentions—still tell me that's true. But the facts and the evidence tell me it is not." What? Granted—I was young; however, this statement confused me. What was he trying to say? He lied? Well, no, not really—that's not what he said. But that's what it meant. In my parents' house, my sister and I would get in far worse trouble for lying than for any particular act of bad behavior. Had the president lied?

And what did he mean by "trading arms"? I had no idea. I'm sure at that time I didn't spend too much energy dwelling on it—at seven years old, I was likely more interested in turning the channel to find better programming (*The Muppet Show*, *Masters of the Universe*, maybe *G.I. Joe*). It was years later that the importance of the president's words—his claiming responsibility and yet not claiming it—would sink in.

As I take time now to look back, I remember not really paying *close* attention to the faces on the nightly news or to what was being said. But I *do* remember the faces. I recall a young Lt. Col. Oliver North standing before a congressional committee, raising his right hand, swearing to tell the truth. Something about trading arms. There it was again: "trading arms." Apparently it was a big deal.

In the last twenty years, there have been many—many!—books written about Ronald Reagan: some glowing, others critical. It would not be an exaggeration to say that the majority would fall into the former category, far fewer in the latter. In today's Republican Party, Reagan is lionized as a transformative president. During the GOP nominating conventions of 2008 and 2012, his name was spoken in reverential terms.

All but forgotten by today's Republicans is the runaway deficit spending of the Reagan administration, the illegal actions undertaken in Iran and Nicaragua, the amiable presidential figure who saluted the US armed services but whose inaction left marines in an untenable situation in Beirut—an ultimately deadly affair that cost some 304 American lives.

Reagan was without question a great communicator. But missing in today's analysis of Reagan is nuance. Context is necessary. There is a children's rhyme that can be instructive, and it goes as follows: "Sticks and stones can break my bones, but words will never hurt me." The song is wrong. Words are powerful (and Reagan surely knew this). Words can move people. They can inspire and can pull at one's heartstrings. "To touch the face of God" still puts a noticeable lump in my throat. Words sometimes command armies. And they can kill.

The purpose of this book is to bring nuance back into the discussion, to take a more honest look at the legacy of Ronald Reagan and of his successors. We are today living with the cost of that legacy. We can remember President Reagan for the kind smile, the important moments shared with (soviet leader) Mikhail Gorbachev, the soaring rhetoric, the "shining city on a hill." But we must also contend with his failures—Beirut, Iran-Contra, Reaganomics.

It would be intellectually dishonest to rest blame for the nation's troubles on one man. No administration can alone bear responsibility for difficult times. The failures of the Reagan administration, though—both economic and from a military standpoint—had sustained repercussions that were further expanded during the presidency of George W. Bush. Indeed, one cannot appreciate the Bush

II presidency or the "war on terror" without analyzing it in terms of a "Reagan restoration." George W. Bush is, by his own admission, a Reaganite. This would have tragic consequences for the nation.

George W. Bush attained the presidency in hopes of exorcising his father's ghosts—in other words, to succeed where his father had failed. The first President Bush failed to win over the more "conservative" element within the Republican Party. He raised taxes. He led the nation, first through diplomatic means and second through military force, against Saddam Hussein—but he did not remove the dictator from power. George W. would not make the same mistakes.

And in this, he proved to be very adept. George W. Bush did *not* repeat his father's mistakes. His mistakes were of a different sort and had far greater implications. Historians have rightly come to see the first President Bush as a man whose pragmatic, cautious approach to things served the nation well, whereas his son's shoot-from-the-hip energy led him to embrace a reckless, ill-informed management of the United States both in economic and foreign policy matters. This is why, in the previous paragraph, I wrapped the word *conservative* in quotation marks. The people who have claimed the word as their own—men like George W. Bush and Dick Cheney—proved to be anything but conservative, whereas the first President Bush (in the pragmatic, cautious temperament discussed) embodied the word as it is truly defined.

The men who today claim to be conservative (politicians like Mike Huckabee, Mitch McConnell, Ted Cruz, and talk radio host Rush Limbaugh) each recall, with admiration and affection, great names of Republicans past: Theodore Roosevelt, Barry Goldwater, and Ronald Reagan. Such men have so distorted the conservative orthodoxy that they cannot see clearly. They are blind to the evidence before them—that the party they have fashioned would never be caught voting for the very men they admire: Roosevelt, Goldwater, and Reagan. In fact, all three have records that—when one takes a hard, honest look— would enrage today's "conservatives."

Things are equally disheartening for today's Democratic Party. In 2008 and again in 2012, the nation voted for "change," electing the first African-American as president of the United States. Barack Obama's 2008 campaign had, in fact, been a referendum on the Bush II years, touting *change*. And yet when one looks closely at the current trend, the disturbing truth must be recognized: that rather than a dramatic split with past practices, the nation has been delivered more of the same.

For example, the use of secret drone strikes during the Obama administration has reignited fierce debate over the role of government and its war-making powers and the need for security. That debate intensified recently, when (illegal) leaks of classified documents detailed domestic spying operations by the NSA. This reopened a heated argument between those who suggest that national security is an end that justifies any means and those who extol the right of privacy. These are old arguments, offering a rehash rather than a "change" in direction.

Defense spending continues to stagger the imagination, and military forces of the United States under President Obama are still faced with deployment into far corners of the globe where American interests are questionable at best. Indeed, as these pages are being written, congress is (at the urging of the president) debating whether or not to approve military strikes—limited in scope, according to the White House—against the nation of Syria. The proposed strikes would preclude "boots on the ground" and would be carried out not against the Syrian government in particular, but in order to "degrade [Syrian leader] Bashar al-Assad's ability to continue to use chemical weapons." While this sounds reasonable from a humanitarian standpoint, one cannot overlook the reality that such strikes would involve the United States (however limitedly) in what is essentially a civil war in Syria, a country that has not—to date—invaded, attacked, or shown aggression towards the United States.

Neither Secretary of State John Kerry (who favors the proposed strikes) nor Libertarian-Republican Senator Rand Paul, of Kentucky (who questions the wisdom of intervention), can know what will happen in response to American action or inaction. The American people have spoken. According to a Pew Research poll, as of September 1, 2013, a solid 48 percent of Americans oppose Syrian airstrikes, while only 29 percent are in favor (23 percent "don't know"). While it would be unsafe to suggest that foreign policy matters should be decided in the court of public opinion, it is hoped that our elected representatives in Washington, DC, speak *for* us rather than *to* us and that they will act with American sentiment and with history—and not simply with partisan rhetoric—in mind.

With unemployment still very much a problem at the heart of our great republic, with defense spending—still—at remarkable levels, and with talk of possible US intervention in yet another troubled part of the Middle East, it is time to press Pause, to take a "timeout." The United States cannot continue (without undermining its long-held values and risking its soul) to be the world's indispensable police force, attempting to solve other nations' problems while ignoring our own at home. This book will argue that it is indeed time, far past time, for the Republican Party to denounce men like Ted Cruz and Rush Limbaugh and embrace the *true* definition of *conservatism*. It is also time for the Democratic Party to shed its hesitancy, to actively engage in a full-throated fight rather than continue to sheepishly call for bipartisan compromise. Such calls are honorable, to be sure; however, Democrats need to accept that which has become increasingly clear to interested observers: that compromise will continue to be a fanciful—unattainable—vision so long as the other party is uninterested in finding common (or middle) ground.

It is time for Americans to call on our elected leaders to *lead* rather than showboat for the cameras, to *govern* rather than play games in hopes of scoring political points before the next election cycle. It is time, far past time, that we—liberals and conservatives alike—call on members of both political parties to (as Ronald Reagan suggested) "check and reverse the growth of government which shows signs of having grown *beyond the consent of the governed.*"

CHAPTER ONE

Inaugural

Ronald Reagan died on June 5, 2004. He was laid to rest in his beloved California. He was, in fact, so closely identified with the state in which he lived most of his adult life that many forget that his were not the values formed "out West" in the California sun but from the mid-West of his boyhood. He was born in Tampico, Illinois—to an alcoholic father and a determined, loving, religious mother—and he reflected the values of Middle America: hard work, belief in God, and a stout love of country. He would embody the American dream in ways that, as a boy, he could not have foreseen.

Or maybe he did foresee a bright future for himself, even as he had to deal with a life that included a father whose troubled relationship with alcohol kept the family forever in search of finding itself "settled." Could he have known or imagined that he would one day become president of the United States?

January 20, 1981, marked the first inauguration of Ronald Wilson Reagan (the little boy from Illinois nicknamed Dutch) as the nation's fortieth chief executive. His candidacy, in which he challenged incumbent democratic President Jimmy Carter, had been a milestone in American political history. Not since the presidential campaign of 1964—in which Barry Goldwater ran unsuccessfully against Lyndon Johnson—had the Republican Party put forth a strictly conservative nominee. During his inaugural address, Reagan issued a clear, conservative agenda for the nation. It is worth extended quotation. He said,

> These United States are confronted with an economic affliction of great proportions. We suffer from the longest and one of the worst sustained inflations in our national history. It distorts our economic decisions, penalizes thrift, and crushes the struggling young and the fixed-income elderly alike. It threatens to shatter the lives of millions of our people.

He continued, "Great as our tax burden is, it has not kept pace with public spending. For decades, we have piled deficit upon deficit, mortgaging our future and our children's future for the temporary convenience of the present. To continue this long trend is to guarantee tremendous social, cultural, political, and economic upheavals."

Thus far, anyone who had ever listened to a Reagan stump speech would quickly recognize the familiar elements of his argument. There were economic problems facing the nation, to be sure, and the government—rather than being a responsible force for fixing the problem—was only making things worse by mismanagement through high taxation and overspending. Further into his speech, Reagan crystallized his argument:

> The economic ills we suffer have come upon us over several decades. They will not go away in days, weeks, or months, but they will go away. They will go away because we, as Americans, have the capacity now, as we've had in the past, to do whatever needs to be done to preserve this last and greatest bastion of freedom. In the pres-

ent crisis, government is not the solution to our problem. Government *is* the problem.

His message? Less taxation and less federal spending. Let hardworking Americans keep more of the fruits of their labor—their earned paychecks (so it was argued)—while putting an end to, or at least reining in, the harmful overspending in Washington, DC. This was a very Jeffersonian argument. The new president wanted to preside over a less-intrusive government, and the idea had great nationwide appeal. With unemployment at a rate of 7.5 percent for the better part of the year 1980 under the Carter administration, Americans were open to a new, or at least to a different, vision. When, during a televised debate with Carter, Reagan asked the audience if they felt they were better off than they were four years ago, he succeeded in presenting the election in its simplest terms.

Now, immediately after being sworn into office, he once again shaped his vision in simple terms. Further government intervention was not the solution to the problems Americans faced—government was the problem. And he intended to act. His stated goal? A balanced budget for the nation by 1984. How could the assembled audience *not* applaud? The former film and TV actor, former governor of California, indeed the "hero from the West," was here to fix things. Reagan liked the role of hero. In the movies, he rarely ever played the villain. Here was his chance to make a difference on a grand stage.

It started out in promising fashion too.

On November 4, 1979, Islamic extremists had taken over the US embassy in Tehran, taking sixty Americans hostage. (What business the United States had in having a presence in Iran will be explored later.) President Carter was painted into an impossible position, wanting to work for the release of the hostages while somehow remaining firm in the government's policy of refusal to ever negotiate with terrorists. The crisis lasted throughout the campaign year of 1980, which spelled trouble for Carter, who came across as a well-meaning man of sound moral character who was in over his head in the Oval Office. The news reports broadcasting footage of the hostages wearing blindfolds and losing weight in captivity were forcing Americans into a state of anxiety and anger.

It was only after Ronald Reagan had been sworn in as the nation's fortieth president that word spread that—after 444 days—the hostages had finally been released. In fact, the timing turned out to be anything but a coincidence. In an effort to add salt to an open wound and further undermine President Carter, Iran's Ayatollah Khomeini had ordered the release of the hostages but reportedly kept the plane they boarded waiting on the airport tarmac until after Reagan's swearing-in. Americans were at once sensitive to the insolent snub to their nation and to the painful experience of their fellow citizens who'd been held hostage, and relieved to have the awful ordeal finally over. And the man at the center of attention? The new commander in chief, Ronald Reagan, who (through no real effort of his own) suddenly looked much more effective than the in-over-his-head Carter.

There would be no need for a Hollywood director—a Spielberg or Scorsese—to intervene. The Reagan presidency had barely begun, and almost on its own, the image of a tough, straightforward, no-nonsense "hero" was quickly taking shape. Just as Herbert Hoover witnessed the political ascension of Franklin Roosevelt to the tune of "Happy Days Are Here Again" in 1933, now Jimmy Carter, after only a single term as president, had to watch gloomily from the sidelines as a new team took credit for a turning of the tides. Americans that day might be forgiven for having imagined "Happy Days Are Here Again" playing in the background during Reagan's inaugural.

It is sad that history has saddled Carter with an impression of ineptness. Jimmy Carter was born in rural Georgia. His was a humble boyhood that was every bit as important in shaping his life and legacy as Ronald Reagan's had been. Both men—in fact—believed in a strong work ethic and in a Heavenly Father watching over the faithful. Their origins were alike, their faith was heartfelt, and their politics overlapped too: both felt that government had a real responsibility to be more frugal with the people's money. He was, in point of fact, a conservative Democrat—not nearly the "tax and spend" liberal (in the fashion of a Lyndon Johnson or a Ted Kennedy) that the Reagan team portrayed throughout the 1980 campaign. Carter had done much in an effort to moderate his party. He called for less waste in government spending and made proposals for less American dependence on foreign oil. In other words, he was the kind of Democrat that conservative Republicans could work with.

The times, however, were not kind to Carter. His term of office was encumbered by the economic problems—inherited from a Nixon/Ford term—of high inflation (as Reagan pointed out in his inaugural), high unemployment, a gas crisis, and finally, the untimely and tragic events of the hostage crisis. Had the "perfect storm" of these several upsets not taken place—all swirling at the same time—Carter might have proven to be an effective president. Such speculation is, however, an academic exercise. The cards, once dealt, are those with which Carter had to contend.

The question on January 20, 1981, was, how would Reagan perform in office? To be sure, Reagan's first and overriding concern was the economy. He knew (1) that economic trouble had been largely responsible for Carter's loss at the polls and (2) his agenda for economic recovery—based on tax reduction and a federal spending overhaul—was something that he was eager to set in motion. It was a philosophy he'd been detailing for years. He was not going to waste time in trying to get things moving.

Detailing for years. One is then forced to ask, How had Reagan handled this agenda—the one he would bring with him into the Oval Office—while he was governor of California? This is an important question and one that too many of today's conservative Republicans tend to either overlook or be ignorant of.

Ronald Reagan had served as California's governor for two terms, from 1967 to 1975. It was a difficult time for America. The war in Vietnam had become an unwinnable nightmare. At home, Martin Luther King Jr. was killed, and the civil rights movement—which had started with such promise—worsened as city after city erupted in violence and disorder. The purported Chinese curse says, "May you live in interesting times." The late '60s was a living-out of that curse.

Reagan proved to be a tough chief of state, sending troops in when the campus at Berkeley was taken over by student protest. While this did not endear him to the younger generation of Californians, most average, middle-income workers (Nixon's "silent majority") approved of Reagan's determined stand as a call for law and order. But what of his fiscal policy? How did Reagan, the Jeffersonian idealist, perform as governor? Journalist Lou Cannon, a Reagan biographer whose books include *Governor Reagan: His Rise to Power* and *President Reagan: The Role of a Lifetime*, answers:

> No amount of budget reductions… could have balanced California's budget in 1967. The cornerstone of Governor Reagan's economic program was not the ballyhooed budget reductions but a sweeping tax package four times larger than the previous record California tax increase obtained by [democratic] Governor [Pat] Brown in 1959.

Governor Reagan oversaw a top income tax rate increase from 7 to 10 percent. The bank and corporate tax rate increased from 5½ to 7 percent. According to Lou Cannon, "An economist who analyzed the tax bill without knowing its political background might conclude that it had been crafted by a New Deal Democrat," rather than the no-holds-barred conservative governor. All told, state revenues—through tax hikes—tripled from fiscal year 1966/67 to 1974/75.

Poor Jimmy Carter. If only he'd been able to better inform the voters during the 1980 campaign of his opponent's true colors. Sadly, voters were less concerned with specifics (say, for example, the actual record of the Republican candidate) than they were ready to hear what they wanted to hear, which, it turned out, was "better times are around the corner." Happy days are here again, indeed.

As the new president, the fortieth chief executive, stood looking out at the crowd that had gathered to listen to and to witness his swearing-in—and as he made promises to the American people that he would usher in a new term of fiscal responsibility and lower taxes—Californians (those with good memories at any rate) must have felt a pang of uncertainty. I'm almost sure Carter did.

CHAPTER TWO

Context

George Bush (not to be confused with his son, George W. Bush) was Ronald Reagan's running mate in 1980 and again in 1984. But before joining Reagan on the Republican ticket, he was himself a primary candidate running for the nomination. It was a bruising primary season, and a crowded one at that. Senator Bob Dole, of Kansas; Senate Minority Leader Howard Baker, of Tennessee; Senator Lowell Weiker, of Connecticut; and US congressman John B. Anderson, of Illinois, all tossed their hats into the ring. The state of Texas was well represented in the Republican primaries too—with CIA director George Bush of course and former Texas governor John Connally also in the running.

It was during the primary season that the term *voodoo economics* was first used to deride Reagan's "supply side" or "trickle down" philosophy. The term originated with—of all people—the man who would eventually share the ticket and become Ronald Reagan's vice president, George Bush. Despite the bumpy beginning to the relationship, it was a successful team-up. In fact, one of the first things Bush told staffers while settling in as vice president was that he would, as veep, support his president, and expected those staffers who worked for him to do the same. He would not tolerate any backstabbing between the two offices. Any disagreements with official White House policy would be kept quiet.

What troubled Bush was not the idea that, if business owners for example were given tax relief, the fruits of a "lighter load" would, in waterfall fashion, "trickle down" (hence the term) to the working classes. No, Bush's problem was with Reagan's math: with the seemingly incongruent call for (1) tax reduction and (2) a simultaneous increase in defense (or military) spending. (I will undertake a further examination of Reagan-era defense spending in chapter 3.) Bush knew that this would not work—never mind the fanciful notion that it could lead, as Reagan proposed, to a balanced budget by 1984. Bush argued that while he approved of a tax cut, the notion that a cut could somehow lead to an increase in revenues (which is what Reagan was suggesting would happen) was ridiculous. Bush called the idea "voodoo economics," and the term stuck in the press. Obviously this didn't do ruinous or permanent damage to Reagan's run for the presidency, and really nothing Bush or any other critic said would shake Reagan's core belief in his limited government / tax relief agenda. However, it was certainly something that must have initially unnerved the presidential hopeful.

No, no ruinous damage here: in the election of 1980, the Reagan/Bush ticket walloped the Democratic Carter/Mondale team.

George Bush was the son of a wealthy East Coast family. His was a privileged boyhood that could not be more unlike Ronald Reagan's. In fact, George Bush was everything that Ronald Reagan pretended to be in the movies: an all-American team player (he played baseball at Andover), a young man who served his country as a pilot in World War II (Reagan served stateside, filming propaganda pictures), and a true-blue Republican (Reagan started his life as a Democrat who voted for FDR). For anyone looking at the political landscape in 1980, it was not Ronald Reagan but George Bush who would have struck potential voters as the genuine article.

Despite their personal or temperamental differences (or perhaps because of those differences), the two men worked well together.

After eight years working alongside each other in DC, Ronald Reagan retired to the California hills and his vice president would become the nation's forty-first president.

Mr. Bush was the first VP since Martin Van Buren (in 1836) to be elected president in his own right (as opposed to assuming the presidency following the death of a sitting president). During his own term, Bush would walk the line between continuing Ronald Reagan's policies and moving away from those policies. He wanted to preside over what he called a "kinder, gentler America." He applied this attitude when dealing with other nations, most especially in working with leaders of the Soviet Union; he also tried to work in a more bipartisan fashion with Congress here at home. His was a less-strident approach to such domestic issues as taxes, for example. While he memorably declared during his 1988 campaign, "Read my lips: no new taxes," he worked with leaders of both parties to fashion an acceptable compromise bill when the economic health of the nation needed a shot in the arm. It has, in fact, been argued in recent documentaries that Mr. Bush's tax bill greatly helped the economy: giving it an injection which—of course—bore fruit during the Clinton years.

Such action would cost him reelection; however, when considering the first President Bush with the 20/20 clarity of hindsight—especially in view of the breakdown of cooperation in today's Washington, DC—one can't help but feel a deep appreciation for his bipartisan leadership.

It is interesting—and terrifically important—to note Mr. Bush's differences with Ronald Reagan, both in terms of personal approach and specific policy, for reasons that would become obvious to a later generation of voters. The proposals made by Ronald Reagan as a candidate during the 1980 primary season (as well as overall approach to governance) would, in large measure, be adopted by a future president of the United States: the forty-third, George W. Bush. While his father proved to be cautious (showing an early hesitation in acceding to the wisdom of Reagan's economic vision), the son would later venture into shaky territory, with disastrous results.

CHAPTER THREE

The High Cost

In 2006, the man who had been Ronald Reagan's secretary of defense—Caspar Weinberger—passed away. Donald Rumsfeld, who was then serving as George W. Bush's secretary of defense, said (of Weinberger), "He left the United States armed forces stronger, our country safer, and the world more free." Not one of the three things Rumsfeld notes can or should be taken as absolute truth. The realities on the ground—in fact—would tend to support an argument to the contrary: that the military under Reagan's (and Weinberger's) watch was left morally weakened, our country exposed to greater dangers, and the world at large made to struggle with the fallout.

This chapter does not reflect an abrupt change in topic from the last. The economy was, as previously noted, Ronald Reagan's overriding concern as he entered the presidency. National defense, like any other operational role of the federal government, falls under the umbrella of the American economy. It is more than just a catchy slogan when supporters of the military say that "freedom isn't free." To—for a moment, and for the purposes of this chapter—set aside the fact that the reference is to the high cost in blood and sweat of our brave servicemen and women, the statement is rather accurate. Freedom is *not* free. In fact, during the Reagan administration, national security became very, very expensive.

While liberal politicians like Ted Kennedy lamented Reagan's tightening of the purse-strings when it came to domestic spending to fund "big government" programs (federal aid to education, for example), those same liberals shook their heads to little effect as the president pushed successfully, time and again, for increased defense spending. From the outset, which is to say even before becoming president, Reagan was a man who (1) saw the world in very stark terms and (2) was determined to make a difference. This, he believed, would involve a strong military posture. Why? Very simply put, Reagan felt that an aggressive American posture had been missing from the geopolitical scene, and he was ready to up the ante in order to confront the "evil empire"—Russia.

Much has been made of Ronald Reagan's anti-communist zeal, and it is true: he was not a half-hearted believer. He was the real deal. One should not make the mistake of viewing Reagan's commitment as either insincere or politically calculated. One has to understand the world as Reagan perceived it in order to appreciate this zeal. Or at least, one must understand the postwar period following WWII. The world Reagan saw was one of absolutes. There was black and white, good and evil, right and wrong. In this context, America was a force for good in the world—and those aligned with the United States were fellow travelers on the side of the angels. Those in opposition were—clearly—evil. This is a rather simplistic view of things, but Reagan was not alone in this.

The policy of "containment" (of containing the spread of communism in the face of soviet aggression) was adopted by the Truman administration at the end of World War II. This policy led to US intervention when the communist forces of North Korea invaded South Korea in June of 1950. It also led, a little over a decade later, to US troops being sent into the jungles of Vietnam—a situation, like the one in Korea, best described as a civil war. While historians rightly applaud Harry Truman for his strong conduct in bringing an end to the Second World War, one must appreciate the scope of failure that the policy of containment left at each succeeding administration's doorstep.

The fault is not Truman's alone. The country as a whole suffered from a sort of identity crisis after WWII. In the minds of many confident Americans, only secret dealings and soviet subversion could account for such disappointments as America's inability to keep China from falling to communism, to keep Korea in check, or to keep Vietnam "free." (Never mind that in each case, the scene on the ground was one of deadly national disagreement—civil war—in which Russian influence was limited, that is, until the United States jumped in.) Americans, like Ronald Reagan, viewed each of these unfolding engagements through the prism of a larger puzzle: as a test of American resolve in a cold war "showdown" atmosphere. Black and white, good versus evil.

The problem is that, in case after case, rather than bringing needed stability to a region, American involvement in someone else's fight has served to further *destabilize* the situation. For example: communist China only entered the Korean conflict after American forces pressed ahead and crossed the 38th parallel. (In point of fact, the Korean peninsula had been ruled by Japan until the end of WWII, when in 1945 Allied forces divided the country between Soviet forces in the North and US forces in the South. Thus, in a way, we helped create the environment, setting the stage for our troubles long before 1950.)

Such nuance though was unfortunately lost on a generation of American leaders, from Truman all the way to Ronald Reagan. When Reagan became president, he took with him to the Oval Office a lifetime of experience. At seventy years old, he'd lived through the tragic valleys (and few peaks) of the Cold War. And as previously stated, he was determined to make a difference. He understood that in order to win a game of cards, a player had to have a strong hand. And if the player attempted to bluff, that bluff had to be believed. The nation, Reagan felt, should have a large-enough military threat to meet Russia at the card table. Reagan was, in a very real sense, ready to practice Teddy Roosevelt–style "big stick" diplomacy.

The big stick—or to continue the card-playing analogy, the cards in his hand—would be an incredible buildup of American missiles to counter the presumed soviet stockpiles. Reagan called for, and received, an expensive push for greater military chest-thumping in the form of short-, medium-, and long-range ballistic missiles. The bluff (one hopes Reagan viewed it this way) was SDI, or strategic defense initiative (which was dubbed "star wars" by the media). He called on American scientists to put their energy and talents into designing space-based defensive technology that could hypothetically counter an attack. Star Wars, indeed. Of course, there was a cost to such endeavors. There is always a cost.

In an article written for the *Baltimore Sun*, June 8, 2004, staff writer Tom Bowman says, "The man who spent World War II in Hollywood, wearing an Army uniform and acting in training films, went on to become the commander in chief responsible for rebuilding America's military might and boosting the morale of troops dispirited by the Vietnam war and its aftermath." Most people can agree: this was a good thing.

Mr. Bowman continues, however, noting, "Reagan presided over the biggest *peacetime* defense buildup in history, from high-tech weapons systems to larger training ranges and military pay increases" (italics added). Here, there are good elements mixed with extremely worrisome aspects. Larger training ranges were very likely put to good use by America's brave servicemen and women. Also, one can assume that many struggling military families were greatly helped by pay increases. But, as noted before, there is always a cost.

Bowman continues, "Still, some critics said Reagan's focus on building up the military's nuclear force… needlessly imperiled world peace and produced huge Pentagon budgets and federal deficits." Later in the same article, Bowman succinctly details the problem. He says, "Between 1980 and 1985, the number of dollars devoted each year to defense more than doubled, from $142.6 billion to $286.8 billion."

Here it would be appropriate to remind the reader of Ronald Reagan's stated intentions throughout his long public career, specifically during the campaign season of 1980 and during his inaugural address. Reagan was committed to a rollback of government spending. "For decades," he said in his inaugural, "we have piled deficit upon deficit, mortgaging our future and our children's future for the temporary convenience of the present." He said that "to continue this long trend is to guarantee tremendous social, cultural, political, and economic upheavals." He was right.

Not to overdramatize the point, but the lauded hero of the conservative movement who promised to rein in government spending did the exact opposite. In fact, he revved the government engine to "full throttle." The total national debt at year end 1981 (Reagan's first year in office) was $994.8 billion; by year end 1988 (his last year in office) it was $2,601.1 billion.

I have several close Republican friends who never miss a chance to chastise and condemn "tax-and-spend liberals." These are good and decent men who applaud thrift and who have honest disagreements with Democratic Party orthodoxy; however, one anxiously awaits the look on their faces (or perhaps the excuses they'll offer) as they are confronted with the specific numbers mentioned above in the *Baltimore Sun* article. Any satisfaction on my part will be short-lived. The fact is that Ronald Reagan, due in great part to his arms race with Russia, never saw or sent a balanced budget to congress.

On October 11, 1986, Secretary General Mikhail Gorbachev and President Ronald Reagan met in Reykjavik, Iceland. It was their second meeting as leaders of the two largest superpowers. (I was seven years old.) Gorbachev agreed that human rights were a legitimate topic for discussion—a first in US/Soviet relations. Then, to the surprise of advisors on both sides, an astounding set of proposals was put forth by the soviet leader, which included shelving (or dismantling) not only a specific class of armaments, but *all* US and Soviet nuclear weapons. History, it seemed, could be made at a beautiful but modest white house situated halfway between Washington, DC, and Moscow.

There was one sticking point: SDI (strategic defense initiative). Gorbachev knew that in realistic terms, the troubled Russian economy would not be able to compete with a space-age arms race. However, he agreed to accept the continued development of SDI so long as Reagan limited the testing of any product of that research to the laboratory (in other words, to agree to keep advancements in scientific storage). Reagan said no.

There would be an arms agreement, but not at Reykjavik. The two nations signed the INF (Intermediate Range Nuclear Forces) Treaty, which eliminated a whole class of weapons systems, in 1987—a year after Reykjavik. Gorbachev's offer for complete dismantling of US/Soviet nuclear weapons remains—to date—a fanciful dream that was sacrificed at the altar of SDI.

From 1984 to 1993 (Reagan's second term through George Bush's single term), approximately $39 billion was spent on the program. The "Star Wars" (SDI) contract the Pentagon had with McDonnell Douglas Astronautics Co., which was estimated at $480.6 million, was dropped—canceled—in 1988.

The high cost, though, of Ronald Reagan's foreign policy adventures was not limited to dollar signs.

CHAPTER FOUR

Beirut

"They had no mission but to sit at the airport, which is just like sitting in a bull's-eye." The quote is from Caspar Weinberger, who was—as previously discussed—Ronald Reagan's secretary of defense. One can read the rest online, at FoxNews.com, in an Associated Press article dated January 30, 2006. "I begged the president at least to pull them back," Weinberger continues, "and put them back on their transports as a more defensible position."

In October of 1983, the United States had 1,800 marines stationed in Beirut, Lebanon. The forces were there on a peacekeeping mission, with approximately three hundred servicemen living in a four-story building at the airport. At 6:22 a.m. on October 23, a truck carrying two thousand pounds of explosives crashed into the marine barracks at the airport. Two hundred twenty marines and twenty-one other service personnel were killed in the attack. It is extraordinarily sad to think that the facts of what happened are so succinct—so neat—as to fit briefly into this small paragraph. What words cannot express though is the human toll, the heart-rending loss of 241 American lives.

Why were they there? This will be examined. Could their deaths have been avoided? If Weinberger's account is to be believed, the sad answer is yes.

Why were we there? Because Israel had an itchy trigger finger following what had been (in all fairness) a season of fear and attacks, and because the United States has had, since the beginning, a stronger-than-necessary relationship with Israel. Indeed, those succinct facts detailed in the earlier paragraph are not the beginning but the near end of the story:

In June of 1982, Israel invaded Lebanon. The Palestinian Liberation Organization (PLO) had claimed responsibility for several attacks previously carried out against Israel, and the situation had gone from bad to worse. Israeli defense minister Ariel Sharon said the Israeli invasion of Lebanon was justified in view of the PLO attacks—never mind the facts that there had only been one recorded Israeli death (thankfully, in each suicide bomb attack, only the attacker was killed) or that the PLO was not the operational head of the Lebanese government (that distinction went to President Gemayel). One Israeli death leading to a full-throttle invasion is, to many minds—including my own—an insupportable overreaction. With America's relationship with Israel feeling the pressure, though, US Marine forces were sent in hopes of calming the tension-filled situation. They were not successful.

Following Israel's invasion of Lebanon, the US embassy in that country sent cables warning Reagan that the scene on the ground was fraught with danger. No additional security measures were undertaken to reinforce the embassy. On the evening of April 18, 1983, the president of the United States spoke in a televised address. Grave reports had been coming in, sketched by news channels all day. The president began his speech, saying, "As you know, our embassy in Beirut was the target this morning of a vicious terrorist bombing. This cowardly act has claimed a number of killed and wounded." He continued, "Just a few minutes ago, President Gemayel [of Lebanon] called me to convey on behalf of the Lebanese people his profound regret and sorrow."

This incident, in which sixty-three Americans—embassy officials as well as CIA agents—lost their lives, took place in April of '83, six months before the marine-barracks attack.

That's a total, in six short months, of 304 American lives lost in an effort to help stabilize a region in the Middle East—part of the globe that has never known real peace. What's worse is that the marines at the airport in Beirut were under orders, by instruction of the commander in chief, not to have loaded weapons (this was done—so the thinking went—in hopes that they would appear as peacekeepers and not be viewed as armed belligerents in a war zone). Secretary Weinberger's analogy of sitting ducks in a bull's-eye is appropriate.

In his book *A Different Drummer: My Thirty Years with Ronald Reagan*, Michael K. Deaver—Reagan's longtime aide—says, "The closest I ever came to resigning... was when we did not react as quickly as we should have during the bombings of Beirut, Lebanon." This is from a man whose close relationship with Ronald Reagan lasted through the California governorship years on into the White House.

Contrast this needless loss of life under (Republican) President Ronald Reagan with the deaths of 4—*four*—Americans in Benghazi, Libya, on September 11, 2012, during the term of (Democrat) Barack Obama. Two of the three attacks are narrowly similar, both having been launched against a US embassy. The differences, though, are substantial. In the case of Beirut, there were warning signs.

It may seem petty to unnecessarily inject politics into the mix, and so one can ask, "Why would the author specify the political affiliations of the two presidents?" Because several weeks after the Benghazi attack, I received a note from a Republican friend of mine (alluded to earlier) in which he voiced support for state department firings and possible presidential impeachment. He said, "This is the biggest scandal in my life... I can't think of one bigger." This last sentence floored me—in fact, it stirred inside the initial thoughts for what would become this book. Perhaps he simply didn't know about Beirut.

The reaction to the events in Benghazi were extremely overblown and will be discussed at greater length in a later chapter; for the purpose of this chapter, though, it offers a clear example of the confused hyper-partisanship in Washington, DC, today. Republicans have become very comfortable accusing the current administration of all sorts of villainy without regard to the hypocrisy that their comments reveal. Reagan is to be exalted—his sins either forgiven or overlooked entirely—while Barack Obama is to be impeached. There is an obvious problem with such heated rhetoric: it wastes time in seeking blame rather than problem-solving, and it is intellectually dishonest.

The loss of any American life in service to his/her nation is something to be deeply regarded; the seriousness of such loss should not be underestimated. Politicians should not use such moments of pain in order to score cheap political points while showboating before television cameras. (Men like Mike Huckabee, who called for the impeachment of President Obama after Benghazi, have offered no truly constructive leadership in such moments.) Whether a marine unit in Beirut or a US embassy worker in Benghazi, every American life lost can and should bring the nation together in (1) a sense of mournful resolve and (2) a determined effort to see that whatever miscues, mistakes, or failures occurred are *dealt with honestly* and possible systemic problems solved in order to avoid future tragedy.

We have seen what an inappropriate response to tragedy can be. What, then, would the opposite be? First, one should look at the overall strategic goals of the political moment. Does the foreign policy offer structure to a weak and hurting global community? More to the point, do the foreign policy objectives serve to strengthen or do potential harm to the United States? It is time the American people take a good, hard look at the initiatives taken across the globe in the name of "national defense." This does not need to be a defeatist or pessimistic exercise. To reevaluate conditions *as they exist* and not as we would like them to be, to take a second look at the cards one is holding before placing a bet—these are reasonable and potentially productive moves.

In dealing with the Middle East, it can be argued that the policies of several US administrations have only served to undermine rather than safeguard American security. In an effort to buttress Israeli interests, American leaders have, time and again, put our armed forces in harm's way. Rather than play to the cameras or to blindly support Benjamin Netanyahu's political interests, American leadership should ask itself the difficult questions. The question "*Should* we be doing A, B, C, or D?" must trump "*Can* we do A, B, C, or D?"

Because we can do a thing does not automatically presume that we must—that we should—do that thing. *Can* is easy. We can. American resolve has been tested before, and we have answered in the positive. *Should* is at issue.

Let's return briefly to Donald Rumsfeld's statement (as quoted at the outset of chapter 3). According to Rumsfeld's glowing eulogy, Secretary of Defense Caspar Weinberger "left the United States armed forces stronger, our country safer, and the world more free." A cursory examination of the events of 1983 does not help support this statement. Did our presence in Beirut make our shores more secure or the situation in Lebanon less dangerous? The answer is clear. Was the loss of 304 American lives avoidable? Yes. While Weinberger "begged Reagan" to change the situation on the ground, he did not resign in protest. He and the rest of Reagan's defense team are complicit in the unfolding horror.

Sadly, Beirut would not be the last time Ronald Reagan's "cowboy diplomacy" pushed American military personnel to stand in the crosshairs. For those who are interested, I will highly recommend

Rachel Maddow's excellent book, *Drift: The Unmooring of American Military Power*. In chapter 4 of the book, she offers a well-researched and invaluable analysis of Reagan's adventure in Grenada (the Isle of Spice). I cannot hope to capture the episode nearly as well as Ms. Maddow does.

Should the United States have dedicated men and women serving in an embassy in Benghazi, Libya? Does our presence *there* make the shores of the United States more secure? Again, the answer—to any reasonable mind—is clear. If Obama is guilty of harmful neglect, then Ronald Reagan is no less so. One wrong does not make a right, and one man's mistakes do not justify the mistakes of another. One would hope, in fact, that we can learn from our past wrong turns. However, to claim that Benghazi represents "the biggest scandal" of a person's lifetime is, I am sad to say, either indulgent—politically motivated—rhetoric, or powerfully naive. I can forgive my friend for his statement (it turns out he *was* unaware of Beirut); however, I do not think that the Rush Limbaughs and Mike Huckabees of the world—who are out there before microphones and cameras calling for impeachment—deserve any such forgiveness.

The families of those lost in Beirut and in Benghazi deserve our love, our support, and yes, our apologies.

CHAPTER FIVE

Reagan and PATCO

For the purpose of full disclosure, because this chapter deals with a union strike, I should begin by mentioning that—for the last eight years—I have worked at Sikorsky Aircraft in Stratford, Connecticut. Sikorsky, for those who may not know, deals with government (as well as commercial) contracts to build helicopters and is a unionized "shop."

There was a shining moment that, for many years, I believed was Ronald Reagan's best moment as a national leader. Today, though I still think that's true, I must admit to being less certain as I once was about the outcome and feeling—overall—more conflicted. It took place in the summer of 1981, six months after Reagan was sworn in as president. The "crisis moment" involved PATCO (the Professional Air Traffic Controllers Organization), which was founded in 1968 and whose members in August of '81—some thirteen thousand—declared an illegal strike. The membership sought better working conditions, better pay, and a thirty-two-hour workweek.

Rather than get bogged down in the details of the specific work of air traffic controllers and whether or not the terms they sought held merit, I will highly recommend the book *Collision Course: Ronald Reagan, the Air Traffic Controllers, and the Strike That Changed America*, by Joseph A. McCartin. The book is well written, is extensively researched, and covers the history of PATCO up to and including the 1981 strike. Here, it should simply be noted that the action taken by PATCO was illegal because it was in violation of Executive Order 10988 (signed into law in 1962 by President Kennedy), which barred federal employees from striking against the government of the United States.

Following the PATCO walkout, Reagan held a press conference at the White House, during which he said, "Let me make one thing plain. I respect the right of workers in the private sector to strike. Indeed, as president of my own union, I led the first strike ever called by that union." (Here, Reagan referenced his time as the head of the Screen Actors Guild.) He continued, "But we cannot compare labor-management relations in the private sector with government. Government cannot close down the assembly line. It has to provide—without interruption—the protective services which are government's reason for being. It was in recognition of this that the Congress passed a law forbidding strikes by government employees against the public safety."

The president then issued a clear, straightforward ultimatum: "It is for this reason that I must tell those who fail to report for duty this morning they are in violation of the law, and if they do not report for work within 48 hours, they have forfeited their jobs and will be terminated."

What followed was a storm of questions from reporters. What would the legal recourse be in dealing with those union members who were on strike? Would the president cancel a scheduled trip to California if the strike continued? One reporter asked, "Mr. President, why have you taken such strong action as your first action? Why not some lesser action at this point?"

The reply was decisive and yet searching in tone. "What lesser action can there be? They are violating the law!"

It was with this last statement (before turning the question/answer session over to the secretary of transportation) that Ronald

Reagan—still very early in his term as president—struck a determined note for law and order. It was, as suggested at the outset of this chapter, a defining moment. While he might sympathize with the air traffic controllers, he was unwilling to negotiate with those who had gone beyond the limits of the law. After the forty-eight-hour deadline, some 11,300 workers who did not return to report for work were fired.

In August 2011, on the thirtieth anniversary of the PATCO strike, Joseph A. McCartin (the author of *Collision Course*) wrote an op-ed in the *New York Times*. He said, "More than any other labor dispute of the past three decades, Reagan's confrontation with… PATCO undermined the bargaining power of American workers and their labor unions. It also polarized our politics in ways that prevent us from addressing the root of our economic troubles: the continuing stagnation of incomes despite rising corporate profits and worker productivity." It is in agreeing with this last statement where I, personally, have become conflicted. Reagan stood up and strongly advocated respect for law and order—an action that I consider one of his finest moments. And yet the outcome as described by Mr. McCartin is unavoidably difficult to wrestle with.

This chapter may seem like a departure from the topics of government spending and military force during the Reagan administration covered thus far in the proceeding chapters. It is. There are reasons, though, for choosing to introduce this unrelated material. I did want to show that there were moments when I loved Ronald Reagan for his determined actions. But—more importantly—there is this: I wanted to introduce a ringing sound bite. Whatever the political disagreements or conflicted feelings one might have about Ronald Reagan's 1981 standoff with PATCO, one important statement should be remembered—and remembered well—as the reader moves on to chapter 6. It is Ronald Reagan's own voice, saying, "They are violating the law!"

CHAPTER SIX

Arming Terrorists

A year ago I was involved in a discussion with several coworkers during which my friend—a Republican—referred to President Barack Obama as the "liar-in-chief." I can't recall the specific topic then being discussed; however, I was not going to argue the merits of my friend's accusations head-on. (This would've been a futile exercise as, in the time I've known him, he has never had anything good to say about *any* Democrat. Nothing I said was going to suddenly change his mind about Obama.) Instead, I took a different approach and challenged him to name for me—if he could—a president of the United States whom we could agree had never lied (so far as anyone knows) to the American people. (Full disclosure: the name that came to my mind was Harry Truman.) I was, on the one hand, delighted with my interesting challenge and, on the other, sincerely curious as to how my friend would answer. He looked up and answered rather quickly with two words: "Ronald Reagan."

I have shared with the reader—in the book's introduction—a number of pieced-together memories: Ronald Reagan's speech to the American people about what he called his Iran initiative, Oliver North standing before a congressional panel before delivering his testimony. I was young then. In the intervening years, I had become a student of American political history. My bookshelves are filled with presidential biographies: Franklin Pierce, Grover Cleveland, Warren

G. Harding, Ronald Reagan. I was therefore thunderstruck by my friend's response. I had challenged him to name a president who had never lied to the American people. My friend was a good deal older than I—one thus assumes he'd be more knowledgeable—and yet I knew he was serious. This left one of two possibilities: either (1) he was unfamiliar with the particulars of Iran-Contra or (2) he was fully versed in the complexities of the affair and still willing to cede Reagan the benefit of every doubt.

Before further comment, a brief synopsis of America's relationship with Iran will be useful. Iran was, for many years, one of our nation's strongest allies in the Middle East under the secular leadership of the shah—Mohammad Reza Shah Pahlavi. In January of 1979 (the year I was born), violent demonstrations led to what historians call the Iranian Revolution, during which the Shah was removed from power and the country was reshaped as an Islamic Republic by the Ayatollah Ruhollah Khomeini. Khomeini and his followers were Islamic extremists; their overthrow of the secular Iranian government was considered part of a "holy war." The United States, meanwhile, was denounced as an evil imperial power whose presence in the region was unwanted, and in November of 1979, Khomeini severed official diplomatic ties, and a number of his revolutionaries seized the US embassy in Tehran. These—the officials working at the embassy—were the hostages Jimmy Carter was unable to successfully free in the remaining year of his presidency (as discussed in chapter 1). In time, more Americans would be taken hostage.

In 1980, the Iran-Iraq War began.

It was at this time, in an atmosphere of high tension and geopolitical upheaval between nations that had once been allied, that Ronald Reagan stepped onto the stage as the newly elected American president. From the outset, there was a genuine wish for a number of things: (1) to strongly condemn terrorist activity undertaken by Islamic extremists against the United States or any other nation and

(2) to explore possibilities, wherever they might exist, of easing the tension and potentially improving relations between America and Iran. The first goal was easily achievable. The second would prove increasingly elusive in theory and problematic in dynamic terms. It was this well-intentioned second goal—a praiseworthy approach to be sure—that would lead the Reagan administration to engage in criminal activity, cover-up, and scandal.

In March of 1984, a religious group connected to Iran kidnapped former army officer William F. Buckley (not to be confused with the famous conservative author), who was working with the CIA in Beirut, Lebanon. (Recall that the Beirut attacks described in chapter 4 had just taken place in the previous year.) An American journalist for the Associated Press, Terry Anderson, was also kidnapped. These events, along with kidnappings of other Westerners, refocused Reagan administration officials' efforts to deal with Iran. In dealing with Iran, however, President Reagan offered a crystal clear imperative: that the United States did not—and would never—negotiate with terrorists. To do so would only embolden future anti-American forces to use similar terrorist methods (hijackings, kidnappings, etc.). What the American leadership needed, it was thought, was a back-channel relationship (like those in the Soviet Union that proved very helpful to Jack and Bobby Kennedy during the Cuban missile crisis) with moderate Iranians who, once Khomeini was either ousted from power or dead, could help guide Iran back into a more "America friendly" status. Once again, this was—at heart—a well-intentioned thought process.

Iran was involved in its war with Iraq and was in desperate need of military supplies. Because Iran was known to be a state sponsor of terrorist activities (the kidnappings in Lebanon, for example), the United States Congress had banned the sale of arms to that nation. A plan was devised, however, to offer sales of needed weapons to Iran in hopes of (1) securing the release of American hostages—both in Lebanon and Iran—and (2) strengthening goodwill between the United States and moderate Iranians. The biggest concern, and a real problem for the United States, would be the potential for weapons—once in Iran—to fall into the wrong hands. There would be little anyone could do to ensure that this would not happen.

Throughout 1984 and 1985, Robert "Bud" McFarlane, Reagan's national security advisor, met with several men in order to get things moving: Adnan Khashoggi, a Saudi Arabian businessman; Manucher Ghorbanifar, an Iranian arms dealer; and David Kimche, an Israeli diplomat and deputy director of the Israeli spy organization Mossad. It was this group that laid the groundwork and executed the plan.

Israel (through Kimche) was brought in for deniability reasons because of the congressional ban on arms sales to Iran. It was arranged that Israel would sell American made TOW (tube-launched, wire-guided) antitank missiles to Iran in exchange for the release of hostages. Khashoggi and Ghorbanifar would handle the money transfer on the "sale" end. Five hundred TOWs would be sold to Iran. In August of 1985, while President Reagan was in the hospital following surgery, McFarlane visited Reagan and discussed the proposed plan. It is important to note, both men have agreed that the discussion took place. According to Bud McFarlane, it was then that the president consented, giving his approval for the official go-ahead.

In December of 1985, Admiral John Poindexter took over McFarlane's post as the president's national security advisor. The Iran initiative continued.

On January 17, 1986, Reagan signed a "presidential finding," which authorized further sales of arms to Iran. The following month, February 27, 1986, one thousand additional TOWs were sent to Iran. No hostages were immediately released.

"Regan told me without hesitation that we had been dealing with Iran for quite a while, and had sold them small amounts of arms, obtaining in the process the release of three hostages." The quote comes from Peter J. Wallison's book *Ronald Reagan: The Power of Conviction and the Success of His Presidency*. Mr. Wallison, it should be noted, is not a Reagan detractor; rather (as we see in the title of his book) he views Reagan as a success. Here, Wallison—who served as the president's legal counsel from April of '86 to March '87—describes a conversation he had with the chief of staff Donald Regan, which took place in November of 1986. Mr. Wallison continues his recollections:

> I said I was not certain about the legality of the activity under the Arms Export Control Act… but Regan said that the Attorney General had been involved in the discussions of the matter from the beginning, so he was reasonably sure that everything was done legally. [Here, Mr. Wallison references Reagan's longtime advisor / attorney general, Ed Meese.]

Note that two important words stand out: *reasonably sure*. Those who were in the know were on record as feeling *reasonably sure* that what they were doing was legal. It is a remarkable disclosure.

Are you *certain* you paid the parking ticket? Well, not really—no—but I am reasonably sure.

In point of fact, the "reasonably sure" statement was an outright lie. Those involved (McFarlane, Poindexter, and associates at the NSC) had jumped through hoops—going so far as to involve Israel—to avoid public disclosure of the transactions. They were well aware that such activity was in violation of Congress's arms ban. In all, some 1,500 missiles had been delivered to an outlaw nation that viewed the United States as an evil imperial power, three hostages were eventually released (others, including William F. Buckley, died in captivity), and $30 million had changed hands. *And what would be done with the proceeds of the secret sales?* Here, one is forced to revisit what was developing on the other side of the globe from an American foreign relations standpoint.

The history of unrest in Nicaragua is too involved to invest deep analysis here. A brief overview, however, will remind readers that a revolution took place in the late 1920s, wherein Augusto Sandino led a rebellion against two formidable opponents: the sitting (American-sponsored) leader Adolfo Diaz in particular and American occupation of Nicaragua in general. Fighting continued as Diaz left power; Anastasio Somoza Garcia took Diaz's place, with the Somoza Dynasty ruling over the next forty-three years. It wasn't until August of 1978 that rebel Sandinistan forces (using the name of the leader who died in 1934) captured the national palace, officially taking power in July the following year.

Ideologically, the Sandinistas were of the Marxist fold, interested in re-creating Nicaragua as a socialist state. And just as Augusto Sandino was, the group was opposed to US intervention in the region. In 1980, the Sandinistas signed economic and cultural agreements with the Soviet Union. These factors, as well as press restrictions enforced by the new government, led the Reagan administration to view the power shift as undesirable and the Sandinistas as a potential threat to security in the region. President Reagan cut off aid, which Jimmy Carter had authorized in hopes of smoothing the power change in Nicaragua.

The Contras, trained in Argentina and operationally equipped in Honduras, was a rebel group in opposition to the Sandinistas. Though there was some evidence that the Contras purposefully targeted civilians, the Reagan administration viewed Contra efforts to overthrow the Sandinistas as a democratic revolution that must be encouraged and given aid. Americans had become increasingly wary of foreign intervention, however, and so, on December 8, 1982, Congress passed the Boland Amendment. This was a rider—

named for the Massachusetts representative who authored it—to a defense appropriations bill. The rider specifically prohibited the use of funds for the purpose of overthrowing the Nicaraguan government. President Reagan signed the bill—Boland Amendment and all—(one imagines he did this grudgingly) into law on December 21, 1982.

The language of the Boland Amendment proved weak, as it had not been specific enough, barring only "the use of funds" in providing aid to the Contras. The CIA continued—with the president's approval—to provide on-the-ground assistance, going so far as to mine the harbors in Nicaragua. Therefore, on August 1, 1984, Congress passed the Second Boland Amendment, which read, "During fiscal year 1985, no funds available to the Central Intelligence Agency, the Department of Defense, or any other agency or entity of the United States involved in intelligence activities may be obligated or expended for the purpose or which would have the effect of supporting—directly or indirectly—military or paramilitary operations in Nicaragua by any nation, group, organization, movement, or individual."

Talk about crossing one's t's and dotting one's i's! There could be no mistake made in reading the Second Boland Amendment—the language was straightforward and its tone forceful. No American aid to the Contras, period. To provide such aid would be in direct violation not only of the will of the American electorate in general (beyond the consent of the governed) but of the Second Boland Amendment in particular.

This is where one catches up to national security advisors Bud McFarlane and John Poindexter (and their National Security Council associates) and the money from the secret Iran transactions. In order to circumvent the system, the funds had to be "redirected." But where? Certain actors had very bold ideas for an answer.

Lt. Col. Oliver North, a deputy director at the NSC who had been involved in what he called the daily "operational aspects" of the arms deals (meeting with Ghorbanifar, for example)—and who reported directly to McFarlane and Poindexter—felt that despite misgivings in Congress, more should be done to support the Contras. Of the reported $30 million that had changed hands, $12 million went to US government reserves. The rest, a sum of $18 million, went to… that's right… the Contras.

Not to put too fine a point on it, but before continuing, let's take a moment to carefully review the facts. The aim was to keep the Iran arms transactions secret because those actions were in violation of the Arms Export Control Act (specifically mentioned by legal counsel Peter J. Wallison in a discussion he had with Chief of Staff Don Regan as described above). To cover their tracks in one illegal adventure, Reagan administration officials engaged in a second illegal act by violating both Boland Amendments, providing financial support—and in some cases small arms (rifles, ammunition)—to the Contras. One must do intellectual cartwheels in order to believe that this was done without at least a passing awareness of the president of the United States. In realistic terms, I believe that for anyone to think that such transactions were made without Ronald Reagan's official—or at least tacit—approval stretches the bounds of believability, educated reason, and imagination.

The public was made aware of the illegal activities following the disclosure of the arms deals by two Lebanese newspapers. At first, the administration sought to hush the reports as nothing more than anti-American blather from unreliable sources. The story, however, was quickly picked up and gaining traction. At some point as news broke, possibly as early as October of '86, Oliver North set to destroying potentially harmful NSC documents.

In an address to the nation on November 13, 1986, President Reagan said, "The charge has been made that the United States has shipped weapons to Iran as ransom payment for the release of American hostages in Lebanon; that the United States undercut its allies and secretly violated American policy against trafficking with terrorists. Those charges are utterly false. The United States has not made concessions to those who hold our people captive in Lebanon, and we will not. The United States has not swapped boatloads or planeloads of American weapons for the return of American hostages, and we will not." With each repetition of the phrase, Reagan stressed "and we will not."

He continued, "Other reports have surfaced alleging U.S. involvement: reports of a sealift to Iran using Danish ships to carry American arms; of vessels in Spanish ports being employed in secret U.S. arms shipments; of Italian ports being used; of the U.S. sending spare parts and weapons for combat aircraft. All these reports are quite exciting, but as far as we're concerned, not one of them is true." *Not one*—this was an overstatement. Some sealift efforts *had* taken place in making deliveries, and spare parts and weapons *had* been sent, though the president was more or less accurate in assessing that reports were beginning to balloon into the realm of the fantastic. Fantastic, though (as it turned out), didn't mean untrue.

He continued, "During the course of our secret discussions, I authorized the transfer of small amounts of defensive weapons and spare parts for defensive systems to Iran. My purpose was to convince Tehran that our negotiators were acting with my authority, to send a signal that the United States was prepared to replace the animosity between us with a new relationship. These modest deliveries, taken together, could easily fit into a single cargo plane." This was a lie (or at the very least a dramatic oversimplification). According to Oliver North's recollections, the sheer scope in terms of number of weapons (approximately 1,500) made the president's comment all but impossible to support. The idea that multiple deliveries of arms—under a veil of secrecy—was anything other than a considerable undertaking was fanciful at best.

A congressional committee—the Tower Commission—was organized to investigate what the president called "exciting" yet "utterly false" reports. In his excellent book, *President Reagan: The Triumph of Imagination*, historian Richard Reeves describes a meeting that took place at the White House on February 11, 1987, between the president and members of the commission. The members involved were Senator John Tower (R-Texas), Edmund Muskie (D-Maine), and General Brent Scowcroft (USAF-retired, Republican, served as military assistant to Richard Nixon and national security advisor to Gerald Ford).

The episode is worth quotation:

> Reagan wanted to change his story about whether he had authorized the first shipment of American weapons and parts from Israel to Iran. Three weeks earlier, he had told the three commissioners that he had known about, and ordered, the shipment in the summer of 1985—as Bud McFarlane had told the commission under oath. Now, he said, he had talked with his chief of staff, Don Regan, and agreed with Regan's testimony that he did not know of the shipment until early 1986. No recording or official note-taking was allowed, but news of the President's shifting testimony leaked to the press within an hour. (Reeves 2006, 378)

On February 25, the men went again to the White House. The president persisted in claiming that his efforts in dealing with Iran had nothing to do with trading arms for hostages, that he would never negotiate with terrorists. It was at this meeting that Scowcroft challenged the president. There was evidence, Scowcroft said, of a May 1986 action wherein Assistant Secretary of Defense Richard Secord "and a plane full of missiles waited on a runway in Israel, waiting for word that hostages had been released" (Reeves, 381). According to Reeves, it was only after being challenged in this way that the president confirmed the commission's analysis: that given the facts on the ground, the deal clearly appeared to be an arms for hostages swap.

In 2012, the American public was drawn into following the real-life trial of Jody Arias, a woman charged with the murder of her former boyfriend, Travis Alexander. As an interested viewer, I tried to follow the proceedings without bias (as a juror would). There is an educated observation, however, that I embrace: that the testimony of an innocent person does not change, as there is only one truth. Changing testimony calls into question a person's credibility. In the Jody Arias trial, for example, Arias first claimed that she was in another state altogether when her former lover was killed. After continued questioning, Arias changed her story, saying that she had spent the night with Alexander and that intruders broke in and killed him. As facts continued to discredit this second story, Arias recanted her earlier testimony and said that she had killed Alexander in self-defense. Arias wanted her story to fit forensic facts, giving investigators three completely different accounts about what took place. This is not what an innocent person does.

As the Tower Commission continued to look into the Iran-Contra affair, the president—as described above in the Reeves passages—sought to change his story, offering shifting narratives of what he knew, when he knew it, and the extent of his involvement. As I and many others did while following the Arias trial, the reader is here invited to make his or her own educated observations.

In March 1987, following several months of silence on the matter as Iran-Contra continued to steal newspaper headlines, Ronald Reagan was back before the television cameras—this time telling his audience (as quoted in the introduction to this book), "A few months ago, I told the American people I did not trade arms for hostages. My heart—and my best intentions—still tell me that's true. But the facts and the evidence tell me it is not."

I did a bad thing and lied about it... sort of.

There is more to the complex series of events that came to be known as the Iran-Contra Affair than I have shared here. There were reports of a Boeing 707 loaded with crates filled with American weapons sitting on a runway in Tel Aviv; of meetings held by Bud McFarlane, Oliver North, and Ghorbanifar during which they were to meet with Iranian moderates who never showed; discussions at the White House between the president, McFarlane, Secretary of State George Shultz (who voiced concerns and outright opposition to the schemes); and CIA director Bill Casey in which the president allegedly said, "I want to find a way to get this done." There are, as detailed in Richard Reeves's book, presidential memos (or "findings") that have Ronald Reagan's handwritten notes in the margins. My own account here has been an effort to give a broad outline of the series of events. For anyone interested in further research, I will highly recommend the books I've drawn quotes from (Wallison and Reeves), as well as *Firewall: the Iran-Contra Conspiracy and Cover-up*, written by Lawrence E. Walsh (who was the independent counsel appointed by a panel of judges and charged with the initial investigation).

During his testimony before the Senate, Oliver North admitted that in the process of illegally dealing with Iran, he *had indeed* engineered a diversion of the proceeds from the weapons sales to aid the Contras. Also in his testimony, he claimed to have forwarded (over a period of time) five separate memos—each involving the particulars of the diversion—to the president but was personally unable to verify that Reagan had received the memos. North was charged with obstruction for initially lying during inquiries about the diversion of funds, as well as for his role in destroying official NSC documents. (The destruction of documents and resulting lack of paper evidence was especially aggravating, in part because the president was thus able to suggest that he was unaware of activities undertaken at lower levels by members of his administration.)

After an unsuccessful suicide attempt in 1987, Robert "Bud" McFarlane pled guilty to four misdemeanors of withholding information from Congress. He was pardoned in 1992 by President George Bush. His successor as Reagan's national security advisor, Admiral John Poindexter, was charged with five counts of conspiracy to obstruct the congressional investigation. He was found guilty; however, a district court of appeals reversed his conviction due to legal questions regarding the immunity he was given during testimony before Congress.

Secretary of Defense Caspar Weinberger was involved as well. Though he denied having material knowledge of the Iran arms sales, his personal notes and diaries (which he attempted to conceal) proved otherwise. Weinberger was charged with five counts: obstruction, making false statements, perjury involving missile shipments, perjury involving knowledge of Israel's role, and making false statements to the Independent Counsel and to the FBI. He was never prosecuted for these offenses, though, because President George Bush issued a preemptive pardon for Weinberger in 1992.

No charges were ever brought against the president of the United States for his role in the Iran-Contra affair (and though I was young, I do not recall Rush Limbaugh turning red in the face and yelling for impeachment). There was apparently too little evidence—perhaps because of Oliver North's efforts at destroying documents—directly tying Reagan to specific planning or that he had full knowledge of any aspects of the affair. The public believed that at his age, Ronald

Reagan (as he himself admitted) was less concerned with specific details of administration than he was with providing overall goals to be achieved. His own words, though, would suggest that he was fully aware of the arms sales: "During the course of our secret discussions, I authorized the transfer of small amounts of defensive weapons and spare parts for defensive systems to Iran. My purpose was to convince Tehran that our negotiators were acting with my authority."

Acting with my authority. The admission is right there.

During our discussion last year, I challenged my friend to name a president of the United States whom we could agree had never lied (so far as anyone knows) to the American people. Ronald Reagan was the last name I thought he'd give as his response.

CHAPTER SEVEN

Morning in America?

In his final message to the American people before turning over the presidency to his successor, Ronald Reagan said, "This is the 34th time I'll speak to you from the Oval Office, and the last. We've been together eight years now, and soon it'll be time for me to go. But before I do, I wanted to share some thoughts." Farewell addresses tend to be reflective, and this one—his last as president—was certainly so. He continued, "It's been the honor of my life to be your President. So many of you have written the past few weeks to say thanks, but I could say as much to you."

"It's been quite a journey this decade," he said, "and we held together through some stormy seas." It was the first of several maritime allusions he would make during the speech. He ended, though, by returning to a subject he'd covered many times before: his vision of America as a shining city on a hill. "I've spoken of the shining city all my political life, but I don't know if I ever quite communicated what I saw when I said it. In my mind it was a tall, proud city built on rocks stronger than oceans, windswept, God-blessed, and teeming with people of all kinds living in harmony and peace… [t]hat's how I saw it, and see it still."

His last thoughts before closing were given to those who, for eight years, embraced his message of smaller government. "As I walk off into the city streets, a final word to the men and women of the Reagan revolution... my friends: we did it. We weren't just marking time. We made a difference." He could not know how far-seeing those words would be. He did indeed make a difference. He pushed Republican orthodoxy further to the right, and in the twenty-five years since Ronald Reagan left office, it has become increasingly apparent that he pushed the whole nation in that same direction. He won the argument.

In a nation of many differing opinions—of political disagreements—the notion that "government is the problem" has become firmly rooted in the soil of our American discussions. Even during the democratic administration of Bill Clinton, there were no *real* attempts (other than, perhaps, the failed attempt at health-care reform) to push back against such thinking and return to an LBJ-style, activist government. Rather, the new argument was for "smarter government." For those who may not believe so, consider this:

On January 20, 1997, during his second inaugural address, Bill Clinton said, "Government is not the problem, and government is not the solution... as times change, so government must change. We need a new government for a new century... one that is smaller, lives within its means, and does more with less." This was different: it was not the "new deal" style argument that twentieth-century democratic administrations had embraced. One cannot imagine, for example, FDR or LBJ saying such things. Clinton continued, "The preeminent mission of our new government is to give all Americans an opportunity—not a guarantee, but a real opportunity—to build better lives."

Clinton's approach was—to be fair—less strident, more nuanced than Reagan's; however, it certainly had echoes of the Great Communicator's focus on self-reliance and responsibility. Without question, it definitely owed more to—and had more in common with—Ronald Reagan's vision of America than it did Lyndon Johnson's. Reagan had succeeded in changing the discussion.

There were other successes too that cannot—should not—be overlooked. When he became president, the national picture that he inherited from a beleaguered Jimmy Carter was rather gloomy. The economy was not at all well. There were gas lines (due to an oil embargo). There were American hostages in Iran. An overall sense of unhappiness with the way the country was headed—if not outright desperation—had taken hold. Perhaps Ronald Reagan's greatest achievement was restoring America's sense of hope in the future. (In his successful 1984 bid for a second term, radio and TV ads proclaimed that, under Reagan's leadership, it was "morning in America.")

Many admirers credit President Reagan with the fall of the Soviet Union. While the arms race certainly did much to push the troubled Russian economy toward its eventual collapse, I would argue that no one person can take credit; rather, it was a number of US presidents—from Kennedy to Reagan—whose firm stands against Russian aggression ultimately bore fruit. Also, had Reagan's successor—George Bush—handled things in a more imprudent manner, the outcome might have been very different, indeed. For example, had he, in his own words, "danced on the wall" as the Berlin Wall was torn down, it would have forced Gorbachev into an impossible position within the Kremlin and may well have led to further hostility between the two nations. If Reagan's posture made the fall of the Soviet Union possible, it is George Bush who is given too little credit for ensuring its peaceful outcome.

We cannot forget, nor can we gloss over, Reagan's failures. To do so would be foolish (and as stated earlier, intellectually dishonest).

The economy did improve; however, the experience was not an uninterrupted climb to greater and greater prosperity. The blue-collar working class as well as those living below the poverty line continued to struggle. Under Reagan's watch, the business executives did rather well. The 1980s were very good for the top 1 percent of Americans. The "trickle down" effect, however, did not occur. The president cut taxes in his first term; however, he actually raised taxes during his second term in order to offset a period of recession.

Though there were finally positive dividends (as mentioned above), the economic fallout from Reagan's arms race with Russia was tremendous. The runaway spending created enormous deficits—a record that is either ignored or conveniently forgotten by today's Republicans. One wonders, how might things have been different had President Reagan embraced diplomacy? If Reagan had—for example—continued the Nixon, Ford, and Carter efforts of détente, could the United States have made progress with the Soviet Union *without* spending many millions of dollars on creating stockpiles of weapons? Judging solely by Gorbachev's behavior in Reykjavik (as discussed in chapter 3), the answer is—very likely—yes.

How did Ronald Reagan perform as commander in chief? The chapters I've dedicated to American foreign policy during his term speak for themselves. If a president is to be judged by the number of battles won, by the lives lost in service to a soldier's nation, by the gains made by such losses, or by whether or not he has made the United States a safer nation, then I contend that Reagan failed us. Forget (for a moment) the Soviet Union. Recall Beirut. Recall 304 American lives snuffed out. Remember the illegal activities of the Iran-Contra affair, in which the United States supplied an outlaw nation with weapons. Remember, especially, the changing testimony of the president of the United States during the Iran-Contra investigations.

And remember that while *any* shipment of weapons made to Iran was illegal at that time under the terms of the Arms Export Control Act, Reagan quibbled over the *size* of the shipments that were made: "During the course of our secret discussions, I authorized the transfer of small amounts of defensive weapons… these modest deliveries… could easily fit into a single cargo plane." *Oh! Well then, in that case, I guess it's all okay.*

And then, his half-baked confession: "My heart—and my best intentions—still tell me that's true. But the facts and the evidence tell me it is not." To this day, there is—somewhere inside me—the six-year-old who heard the president and is still trying to understand the meaning of the "confession." In truth, at thirty-four years old, I still don't understand how America heard those words, shrugged collectively, and said, *"Oh! Well then, in that case, I guess it's all okay."*

The fact that Ronald Reagan's stated goals (less government spending, for example) are so radically different from the actual record, and that his record is ignored by admiring "conservative" fans, leaves me groping for a way to put his presidency in perspective. To honestly grade his performance is to—at the same time—call attention to an extraordinary hypocritical tendency in the current Republican Party.

His is, at best, a mixed legacy. It is a legacy that would eventually find further development—and failure—during the administration of George W. Bush.

CHAPTER EIGHT

Thinking about George

Depending on whom you ask, you may get differing answers to the question, Who was the nineteenth president of the United States? The same is true when inquiring about the forty-third.

George Walker Bush, the son of the man who served alongside Ronald Reagan, entered the Oval Office as the nation's forty-third president on January 20, 2001. He did so following the most turbulent election since 1876. In that election—between Republican Rutherford B. Hayes, of Ohio, and Democrat Samuel Tilden, of New York—several states (including Florida!) were in doubt, leaving the results to remain undecided for months before being settled (in Hayes's favor) by an electoral committee. The election of 2000, between George W. Bush and Al Gore, also involved disputed votes (and Florida!) and was no less divisive. There are people who, today, still believe that the election was taken from Gore—that he was the nation's forty-third president.

The campaign season leading up to the election of 2000 hadn't exactly been a picnic. Many—myself included—were initially underwhelmed by the choice of George W. Bush to head the Republican ticket. (During the primary, I voted for Senator John McCain and had the opportunity to shake his hand when he visited Sacred Heart University.) In what should have been an especially telling moment, Bush—who was feeling pressured to dispel the impression people had of him as a lackluster "C student" mind-set—was challenged to name foreign leaders of several nations. He had trouble doing so. *Yikes!*

Gore had his problems too. Whether or not this matched the man's true colors, Gore was seen as dull, as academic and cold—a sort of aloof political statue. Bill Clinton had amazed voters with his capacity for sympathy (most famously noted in the "I feel your pain" quote). It was a political skill his vice president seemed to lack. While on the same stage during their debates, Gore was unable to match George W.'s image as "the kind of guy you'd like to have a beer with." This seemed to give Bush a real leg-up; however, one wonders how much damage this *actually* caused Gore's campaign. In any case, it all led to an election that was—as noted—incredibly divisive.

It was a difficult way—under a cloud of hurt feelings and rumors of voter fraud—for anyone to assume the presidency. Because the election had been so stormy, President Bush promised he would be "a uniter, not a divider." Many Americans, even those who did not vote for him, hoped that Bush would succeed in uniting the country. For a time he did. The new president started his inaugural address by saying, "As I begin, I thank President Clinton for his service to our nation, and I thank Vice President Gore for a contest conducted with spirit and ended with grace."

Further into the inaugural, in a moment reflecting his deep personal faith, President Bush said, "Many in our country do not know the pain of poverty. But we can listen to those who do. And I can pledge our nation to a goal: when we see that wounded traveler on the road to Jericho, we will not pass to the other side." These were very caring words. Whatever one may think about the man, George W.'s faith—like Ronald Reagan's anti-communist zeal—was and is genuine. It is one of the very best parts of his character. And yet, the moment was meant to address the sin of suffering (in the form of what he called deep, persistent poverty). As the new leader not only of the nation but of the Republican Party in particular, he was speaking more to active civic engagement, church-based initiatives, and community commitments rather than for government intervention on behalf of those in need. The "wounded traveler" was not about to be given a free helping hand from a new Lyndon Johnson; rather, he would see less Washington-driven legislation and a push for community-led charitable responses. It was an important distinction.

I was (at that time) a registered Republican who, having gotten over John McCain's primary loss, voted for Mr. Bush. His message of wanting to embrace the goal of greater personal responsibility in the country resonated with me. But as the Bush II presidency began, I was, admittedly, less than impressed. I recalled the soaring words Ronald Reagan delivered; the careful way the first President Bush watched German reunification without bragging and beating his chest triumphantly; the caring, hopeful voice Bill Clinton gave to ordinary Americans who wanted to work hard, earn a decent wage for their efforts, and send their kids to college. In the first few months of the Bush II presidency, the "new guy" in the Oval Office seemed to lack a vision for what he wanted to do. He seemed, in fact, to be living up to the "C student" image. The few speeches he delivered—apart from the inaugural address—made me wonder about his speechwriting staff. I missed Peggy Noonan (who'd written many speeches for Reagan).

There were significant successes early on, to be sure. One move I especially liked was the new president's choice for secretary of state—Colin Powell, a man whose sterling reputation and strong character were unimpeachable.

I also had reason to applaud his choice for a running mate. I had no deep understanding of the man or of his views, but I had a peripheral awareness that Richard "Dick" Cheney had served in some capacity during the Ford administration, and I had always liked and respected Gerald Ford. (Cheney was Ford's White House chief of staff. He went on to serve as secretary of defense under the first President Bush—another man I respect.) Donald Rumsfeld was, I believed, another inspired choice; he was another Ford man (he served both Ford and Bush II as secretary of defense). Ford was no radical; in point of fact, he had been a voice of clear thinking and pragmatism as president. To see such men—Ford men—surrounding the new president left me feeling hopeful.

The economy was doing well. We had, as a country, shaken our old Cold War attitudes in dealing with Russia. After eight years of Ronald Reagan—during which personal religious beliefs kept the president from engaging the problem of AIDS (which was then seen as a "gay disease")—and a single George Bush term where he'd been defeated for reelection not so much by Clinton but by voices of the extreme element of the Republican Party, I looked forward to having a Bush II presidency as he himself described: one that would unite the country rather than offer further division, a "Ford restoration" of sorts.

Then, in September 2001, everything changed.

Americans—and people around the globe—embraced President Bush as he carefully led the nation in the first hours and days following the attacks. The Queen sang the American national anthem at Buckingham Palace; on September 12, French newspapers announced, "We are all Americans." In what I regard as being the most significant moments, Russian president Vladimir Putin called the attacks a "blatant challenge to humanity," while German chancellor Schroeder said that the attacks were "not only attacks on the people in the United States, our friends in America, but also against… our own freedom, against our own values… which we share with the American people." With such tributes of brotherhood coming from

Russia and Germany—two nations that shared with us a history not of peace and harmony but of animosity, distrust, and war—I admit I was moved.

We can each recall the moment when, while visiting Ground Zero, President Bush stood atop the rubble of the World Trade Center alongside firefighters and rescue workers. When someone in the back of the crowd called out "We can't hear you," his response (through megaphone) was powerful. He said, "I can hear you! The rest of the world hears you. And the people who knocked these buildings down will hear all of us soon!" Resolve. Defiance in the face of horror. It was an electric moment—one of the president's best. Maybe he didn't need Peggy Noonan; his own sense of self was working out pretty well.

I remember being rather pleased at that hour with having voted for the man.

At that moment, the president of the United States had a real chance to unite. To succeed as few others had in working to fashion a better world. To take the clay that was the chaos of New York and DC and mold a more united group of nations. (Woodrow Wilson experienced such an opportunity in Paris following the conclusion of World War I.) The goodwill was there: "We are all Americans." In the days that followed, however, decisions were made that would completely unravel that sense of unity.

My thoughts regarding Dick Cheney and Donald Rumsfeld would come back to haunt me. The whole nation would—in time—be haunted. Yes, they had been Ford men. But neither man was anything like his former boss. David Gergen—who worked as an advisor to presidents Nixon, Ford, Reagan, and Clinton—called Ford "the most decent man [he] knew." Gerald Ford had been a magnanimous consensus seeker; however, his former lieutenants, Cheney and Rumsfeld, were political gorillas. (In a conversation with his chief of staff, H. R. "Bob" Haldeman, Richard Nixon called Rumsfeld a "ruthless little bastard." Considering the source, the anecdote is quite revealing.) Altogether, their efforts to make the case for—and later to justify—war with Iraq (and to somehow tie that war with the 9/11 attacks) would cost many millions of dollars and untold American and Iraqi lives.

I have a tattoo on the inside of each forearm. One is of a sentence—in her handwriting—lifted from a letter my maternal grandmother wrote me ten years ago, while I was living in Georgia: "I think of you every day." Grandma, who passed away in 2010, was my political companion, and she is still with me. The other tattoo is of the Green Lantern symbol, revealing to the world that I am what some may call a "comic book nerd." In comics, as in science-fiction books and films, a topic that is often explored is the possible existence of alternate realities. Writers—including Newt Gingrich—have written what-if books that examine alternate histories of the Civil War. (What if Lee had done X, Y, or Z?) It is an endlessly fascinating thing to contemplate what-if.

The Bush II presidency will be examined in the following chapters. Whatever political views a person may hold—conservative or liberal, whether you see George W. Bush as hero or villain—there is one absolute: his administration was a significant one. It is highly unlikely that his time in office will fade into obscurity along with the terms of Grover Cleveland, for example. That said, the second President Bush left the United States with many unresolved what-ifs. When historians look back to the stormy election of 2000, many rather absorbing questions emerge. One is forced to ask, In an alternate reality, what would President Gore have done differently? How would he have dealt with the "wounded traveler on the road to Jericho"? Perhaps more importantly, how would President Gore have reacted to the events of 9/11?

CHAPTER NINE

Bush's Benghazi?

On August 6, 2001, President George W. Bush received—during his daily briefing—an intelligence report with terse language that said, "Bin Laden determined to strike in U.S."

What's more, according to an article by Kurt Eichenwald that appeared in the *New York Times* on September 10, 2012, this was not the new president's first briefing on the topic. The existence of several briefings prior to the August 6, 2001, document, according to Eichenwald's report, offers evidence of "significantly more negligence" by the Bush II administration in addressing US security concerns than previously imagined by many Americans. In fact, CIA officers informed Bush of reported threats as early as May that year and continued to press the issue during meetings in June (22 and 29) and July (9).

On May 1, 2001, the CIA told Bush that they had intel of "a group presently in the United States" that was planning unspecified terrorist activities. The June 22 statement suggested that according to reliable evidence, a possible threat was "imminent." No initiatives were taken to increase security details in the nation's airports, bus depots, or subway terminals. No statements were issued from the White House in an effort to inform the public of CIA concerns. Why needlessly alarm people—so the thinking went—without explicit proof? (Vice President Cheney's personal reluctance to rely on CIA intel, in fact his outright distrust of the agency, will be explored in chapter 10).

As early as May. Twice in June. Again in July. And then August.

"In the aftermath of 9/11," according to the report, "Bush officials attempted to deflect criticism that they had ignored CIA warnings by saying they had not been told when and where the attack would occur."

Dear Mr. Bush, we at the CIA have it on good authority that Colonel Mustard (who, according to our sources, will be wearing a yellow cardigan) plans on killing the maid in the dining room two days from Thursday. He will use the candlestick. If only the CIA warnings had been so written, perhaps *then* the president would have done something? Sarcasm aside, this was the basic defense offered above.

I am typically not one to kick a dead horse; however, I feel compelled to take the opportunity and refer the reader to observations made in chapter 4. In September 2012, an attack was carried out against the United States embassy in Benghazi, Libya. Much has been made of the fact that the Obama administration failed to provide the embassy with extra security in the hours leading up to the attack. Still others in the conservative media (Sean Hannity, Rush Limbaugh, Glenn Beck) feel that President Obama, (Secretary of State) Hillary Clinton, and National Security Advisor Susan Rice each provided misleading—or outright false—accounts of (1) the timeline of initial hostilities in Benghazi and (2) the catalyst for the attack.

Whatever the cause of the attacks, or when they began, the eventual outcome remains the same: that 4—*four*—Americans were killed. It was a tragic event. And as I suggested in chapter 4, the loss of *any* American life in service to his/her nation is an important moment that cannot—should not—be brushed aside and left unanswered. The gravity of the situation is clear. (This is especially true in the hearts of those who still have loved ones actively serving in the armed forces.)

That said, I echo my assertion that the Republican response to the event in Benghazi far outweighs the true gravity of the moment. For those who are overcome with a *genuine* concern over the Benghazi scandal, I will ask, are you as deeply outraged over George W. Bush's inaction in the days—actually, months—leading up to the attacks on September 11, 2001? I would hope—sincerely—that your reaction to Benghazi is heartfelt and not simply an example of partisan venom aimed at the current occupant of the Oval Office.

Dear Mr. Hannity, may I ask, in light of the evidence that he twiddled his fingers absently while terrorists entered this country and engineered their sinister plan, why did you not call for the impeachment of President Bush? Surely, his failure to enact extra security measures before 9/11—in which, altogether 2,977 people were killed—is grave enough to warrant your just outrage. Sadly, Mr. Hannity, I have reason to believe that your reaction to Benghazi *is* simply an example of partisan venom.

That goes for you too, Mr. Limbaugh.

CHAPTER TEN

The Contest

On September 11, 2001, I was a student at the University of Connecticut. It was a Tuesday, which meant that I was scheduled to attend math class. I've always had trouble with math. I woke, took a shower, and went downstairs to find my dad watching the news. An airplane had apparently crashed into one of the towers at the World Trade Center. I sat and watched the live coverage. I noticed a small speck in the background and watched as it came closer and closer. I saw—in real time—the second plane rip through its target.

"There were about thirty of us standing around, and as soon as the second aircraft smashed through the second tower, everyone said, 'Bin Laden.'" The quote is from former CIA field officer Gary Schroen, given during an interview for the PBS news program *Frontline*.

"Everybody assumed that it was Al Qaida because the operation looked like Al Qaida, quacked like Al Qaida, seemed like Al Qaida," according to Condoleezza Rice, who was President Bush's national security advisor. Secretary of State Colin Powell—who was in Lima, Peru, at the time of the attacks—immediately returned to the United States. In describing his trip back, Powell said, "I had all that time to think about what happened and about what it was going to mean. Clearly, America was under assault, serious assault."

Everybody assumed, according to Dr. Rice, *that it was Al Qaida*.

Not quite everybody, as it turned out. That very day—with smoke still rising from Ground Zero in New York, the Pentagon, and from a quiet Pennsylvania field where a third airplane was forced down—Donald Rumsfeld dictated a memo to a staffer, which read, "Judge whether hit SH at same time, not only UBL." *SH* was shorthand scribble for Saddam Hussein, the dictator of Iraq. *UBL* (though misspelled) was referring to Osama Bin Laden.

Though later classes held at Uconn were cancelled, the morning schedule was uninterrupted. While I sat in math class with fellow students, discussing—in near disbelief—what we had seen and heard that morning (and not getting anything done in the way of actual classwork), Don Rumsfeld, Deputy Secretary of Defense Paul Wolfowitz, and certain other high-ranking officials in Washington, DC, were already focusing their efforts at connecting the dots in a way that would allow the United States to "go after" Saddam Hussein.

Former CIA officer Michael Scheuer, who is now an adjunct professor at Georgetown University, offers a rather sharp analysis. Scheuer says, "Mr. Wolfowitz, Mr. Rumsfeld, Mr. Cheney—all cut their teeth in the Cold War, in the contest between nation-states. They're not comfortable with thinking that the world's greatest power can be threatened by a couple of Arabs with long beards squatting around a desert campfire in Afghanistan. It doesn't register." This, perhaps, shines a revealing spotlight on the psychology behind the line of thinking that took place in the first few hours following the attacks.

Rather than simply gather information and launch a targeted assault on the group—or groups—responsible, the Unites States had to (so the thinking went) address certain countries that may have played a role or somehow been involved. This second initiative would, of course, involve a greater military operation than the first. No worries. For Donald Rumsfeld (as we've already seen), Iraq—or, more specifically her leader, Saddam Hussein—was "target number 1" on a list for such consideration.

It was decided that once he was back in Washington, President Bush (who had also been in a classroom that morning, in Florida) would make an address from the Oval Office. This would be an attempt to show that things were still running, that the terrorists behind the attacks had not brought the nation to a standstill. They had. But it was important to show the outside world an America pulsing with determined strength. Defense Policy Advisor Richard Perle, who was of a like mind with Rumsfeld, had admitted that he spoke that afternoon with White House speechwriters in an effort to affect the language of the president's address. He wanted to include language that would allow for decisions—whether made in the immediate future or down the road—that would involve the greater strategic aim discussed above (namely, to allow the United States to target nations that were deemed "state sponsors" of terrorist activity).

That night, the president told an American audience—as well as people listening in far corners of the globe—that America had been badly hurt, but that the country was far from shrinking into despair or retreat. He began his speech, saying, "Good evening. Today our fellow citizens, our way of life, our very freedom came under attack in a series of deliberate and deadly terrorist attacks." He continued, "A great people has been moved to defend a great nation. Terrorist attacks can shake the foundations of our biggest buildings, but they cannot touch the foundation of America. These acts shattered steel, but they cannot dent the steel of American resolve."

It set an important tone.

He continued, "The search is underway for those who are behind these evil acts. I've directed the full resources of our intelligence and law enforcement communities to find those responsible and to bring them to justice. We will make no distinction between the terrorists who committed these acts and those who harbor them."

There it was. The words necessary to engage in an effort whose scope would be broadly outlined. The American response to September 11 would not be a limited engagement with specific actors (i.e., Al Qaida). Only hours after suffering the biggest defeat since Pearl Harbor, the president of the United States, the vice president, the secretary of defense (Rumsfeld), the deputy secretary of defense (Wolfowitz), and other lower-level government agents set the country on a dangerous course: one that held real potential to expose American military families to greater levels of conflict than facts on the ground necessitated.

But there was still room for uncertainty in the minds of people listening that night. What did the president mean when he alluded to "those who harbor them"? Which specific countries did he have in mind? He did not say—not that night. In fact, most Americans woke up the next morning—September 12—still not knowing who was responsible for what happened.

I know that, for me, it felt as though I had dreamed the events of the previous morning. In my mind—and in the minds of most people of my generation who had not lived (as our grandparents had) through WWII—war had always been a distant thing. Black-and-white photos. Color scenes on TV of a place far away in a desert where men and boys threw rocks at one another and fired rifles at tanks. Dust-covered men and women running through streets that looked alien and unforgiving. I can easily recall pictures of demonstrations held in such uncaring streets (in 1979) in which Iranian citizens burned a straw doll of the Ayatollah Khomeini in effigy. Naked, burning, tortured streets. In such scenes, those streets looked nothing at all like the streets of New York City. Until 9/11.

If the president and his cabinet did have a knee-jerk type of reaction to the events of 9/11, who could blame them? The horror of what we witnessed at a distance—through our television screens—and of what others who were there actually experienced was incredible. On the most basic level, the human instinct was to do one of two things: to either ball up one's hands into fists or shrink reflexively into a retreating posture. Fight or flight. We cannot ask our leaders to be anything other than human. And yet, they have to be.

They have to be. They have to make hard decisions in hard times. They are asked to do so by a free people who vote into office representatives—people who will speak for us. It may not be fair to ask those representatives to be better than us, but that is what we do. We tolerate certain behaviors in our own neighborhoods—marital infidelity, for example—that we condemn if exposed in Washington, DC. It may not be fair, but it is what we do.

That said, the days that followed the 9/11 attacks found certain powerful men in Washington, DC, acting especially childish. In what can best be described as a middle school–style "[crude term] contest" (hence the name of this chapter), Vice President Cheney, SoD Don Rumsfeld, and Deputy SoD Paul Wolfowitz each tried to present the president with the best case for having the Pentagon (the military)—coincidentally under the purview of Rumsfeld—shoulder the official responsibilities of the "war on terror." Each man wanted to have greater direct control over how the war would be waged than he would have if the operational, on-the-ground details fell instead to the CIA.

Dick Cheney distrusted the CIA, which is perhaps the biggest reason for his wanting greater control. In part, he blamed the CIA for failing to predict or stop 9/11. His distrust, though, goes back further: to his time as Gerald Ford's chief of staff. He felt then that the CIA had grossly underestimated Russia's nuclear capabilities. During the early 1990s, Mr. Cheney served as secretary of defense under the first President Bush. He believed that the CIA failed then too (for having missed signs of Saddam Hussein's potential to pose a threat in developing weapons). Basically, he believed that the CIA could be counted on to be a day late and a dollar short when it mattered.

The president's "those who harbor them" statement during his 9/11 speech seemed to indicate that Cheney (and company) would have little difficulty in selling their point of view. But the Pentagon, it turned out, had no real plan of how to deal with Al Qaida. The CIA, however, had rather impressive amounts of intelligence (gathered over a period of many years) on Al Qaida and on the country where Al Qaida was known to "hide out": Afghanistan. If there was ever a need—that is to say, if national security ever called for an Afghan mission—the CIA was prepared. Agent Gary Schroen, for example, had worked in the late 1980s as the agency's station chief in Kabul, Afghanistan, and had led CIA efforts throughout the '90s directed at capturing Osama bin Laden. If there was one group whose advice was critical for the president to consider at this time, it was CIA director George Tenet and company in the Central Intelligence offices in Langley, Virginia.

J. Cofer Black, a CIA operative who was made director of the agency's Counterterrorism Center (CTC) in 1999, said, "We had been working on this for years. Where everybody else is looking for their maps on Afghanistan, we were ready to rock, ready to roll." According to Black, things started moving quickly on September 11, when "George Tenet said 'Okay, update the plan, have it ready by tomorrow.'"

Michael Scheuer, who was quoted earlier and who worked with Cofer Black in the CTC, describes Black's enthusiasm: "He said 'we're gonna put their heads on pikes and we want flies crawling across their dead eyes.' Y'know, that kind of headquarters hero talk."

A meeting that included the president, vice president, Rumsfeld, Wolfowitz, Secretary Powell, Condoleezza Rice, CIA Director Tenet, and others was held at Camp David that first weekend following the attacks. The CIA put forth its plans for attacking Al Qaida in Afghanistan. The discussion, led by Paul Wolfowitz, then turned to whether Iraq should be involved. The CIA argued against such conclusions being made, that there was no evidence supporting Iraqi involvement. Director Tenet had, in fact, ordered an agency-wide search going back ten years in the files, looking for any information that would suggest a relationship—direct or indirect—between Al Qaida forces and Iraq. The search had produced no hard intelligence. This should have been enough to—at least temporarily—hush voices that were whispering "Iraq, Iraq." The Camp David meeting ended with the president telling those gathered that he would think over the various proposals and have answers Monday morning.

His decision must have stung: the CIA would take the initiative. Iraq was put on the back burner. But Cheney and Rumsfeld would eventually have their way.

CIA operatives—including Gary Schroen—entered Afghanistan in late September 2001 and hit the ground running so-to-speak. They worked with local forces—linking up with anti-Taliban forces, distributing money and small arms weapons. Once the groundwork had been laid, specific military strikes would proceed. That is, the CIA mission "in country" would be joined (if all went according to plan) by Donald Rumsfeld's military forces.

Things did not go according to plan.

"We were there for just about a month by ourselves," recalls Schroen. They were waiting for the military backup that the planning had called for. The CIA complained that Rumsfeld was dragging his feet. It was only in mid-October, after Donald Rumsfeld was told that he—and the Pentagon—would oversee the CIA operations, that special forces moved into Afghanistan.

It is fairly extraordinary: the United States had been attacked, thousands of men and women killed, and the men in charge—those closest to the president: the VP, the secretary (and deputy sec) of defense, and the CIA director—were engaged not in a hard-hitting attempt to combat those responsible for 9/11 but in a "[crude term] contest." Some may find it trivial—perhaps even an example of partisan sniping—to devote energy discussing that particular time in our shared history by combing over the backroom politicking that took place. I admit; there is something to that argument. However, I submit that it is not an irrelevant topic. Far from it. *How* decisions were made at that critical point in time is just as important as *the reasons* they were made. And the outcomes that flowed from those decisions were of ultimate significance.

In the following months, operations in Afghanistan looked to be proceeding slowly but successfully. Many Al Qaida members were captured; those that escaped capture fled into the mountain regions. US Special Forces set to routing sympathetic clusters one village at a time—gaining ground and then falling into holding patterns. It was war just as wars had long been fought—typically one nation at war with another nation—fighting to control territory. It was not the kind of war that the situation called for, however, because we were not at war with a specific country (in this case, Afghanistan). We were dealing instead with a new kind of threat: an enemy that was not tied to any one region or country. A moveable enemy, with sympathetic groups—and individuals—scattered in pockets around the globe.

As I've said, I was only a college student at that time. I had not served in any capacity in the armed forces and had not attended any military academy. And yet in my mind, it was evident—even then—that in order to meet the new type of challenge and engage a new kind of enemy, the United States had to rethink its strategic vision for war. We didn't. And so the early successes in Afghanistan developed—over time—into a sort of standstill, with US troops maintaining gained territory ("freed villages") while dealing with occasional, sporadic flare-ups.

Meanwhile, the political landscape back in Washington continued to bubble and churn with efforts to find something. CIA analysts dug through available reports and made inquiries through multinational sources (per repeated requests from the White House) in hopes of gathering information on possible Iraqi links to Al Qaida. No reliable leads were discovered. At the same time, the Defense Intelligence Agency—or DIA—(the info-gathering division at the Pentagon) organized its own investigations, hoping to succeed where the CIA had so far failed in finding potential links. One episode in particular is worth noting:

In December of 2001, a three-day meeting was set in Rome between several DIA officials and Manucher Ghorbanifar—yes, *that* Ghorbanifar—in hopes of uncovering prospective leads. Ghorbanifar, the man with whom Oliver North had dealings in the 1980s during the Iran-Contra affair, was the same Iranian arms dealer whom the Congressional Committee investigating Iran-Contra described as "an intelligence fabricator" who should be regarded as "untrustworthy." Yes, by all means, let's meet again with *him*.

The DIA/Ghorbanifar meeting involved discussions of secret offers from various shady characters in Iran who were—according to Ghorbanifar—reportedly interested in providing information. Ghorbanifar, it was suggested, hoped to be paid for his role as middleman. When news of the meeting broke, a Senate hearing was convened, during which Donald Rumsfeld himself called the affair insignificant. No reliable info was exchanged. Rumsfeld admitted that "nothing of substance or of value" had been gained.

This was how the "war on terror" was developing (in its embryonic stage, so to speak) during the first charged—highly caffeinated—months after 9/11. The president of the United States, only months into the first year of his term and dealing with an impossibly horrific new challenge, struck an important tone of strength and defiance in the face of evil. His 9/11 speech *was* good. Vice President Cheney and his old ally from Ford days Don Rumsfeld were involved in (1) the "[crude term] contest" with CIA Director Tenet and (2) a resolute effort to find Saddam Hussein's fingerprints somewhere in the rubble of New York and DC. And US forces were settling into the beginning stages of "securing" Afghanistan.

Let's return briefly to the always intriguing question of "What if?" Imagine—for a moment—that those who saw the benefits of waging a more limited war on terror won the argument. Rather than employ America's full military resources in a conventional "boots on the ground" type campaign, the United States might have led several finely focused raids on Al Qaida compounds in Afghanistan (and wherever else intelligence steered us). Rather than become bogged down in a war over securing gained territory, we might well have dealt a crippling blow while committing less capital and suffering less loss.

Imagine if George Tenet—rather than Dick Cheney and Don Rumsfeld—had enjoyed greater access to the president's ear. Might President Bush have been compelled by his arguments that the United States need not invade Iraq? It is entirely possible that—had our military muscle not been divided between two war fronts (Afghanistan and Iraq)—Osama bin Laden could have been brought to justice for his crimes a decade sooner. That is a powerful what-if.

The byzantine "[crude term] contest"—waged between VP Cheney and the Pentagon in one corner, and Tenet's CIA team in the other (with Ghorbanifar thrown into the mix for good measure)—was only the unhappy *beginning* of what would be a long, protracted war (eventually led, as we all know, on two fronts) that would have a staggering cost: many, many millions of dollars and—worse—the lives of countless brave servicemen and women. Though it is a distressing thing to consider, Al Qaida terrorists must have relished the self-inflicted body blows the United States leadership so recklessly dealt their own armed services from the get-go.

CHAPTER ELEVEN

Patriot Games

Following the recent disclosures by intel leaker Ed Snowden, members of the Republican Party have had a sort of collective conniption, losing their minds and falling all over one another—each trying to shout loudest in protesting the government's activities in domestic spying. The National Security Agency (NSA) had collected e-mail and cell phone data in an effort to ferret out potential national security threats. To be fair, both parties have taken issue with NSA efforts; however, it is Republicans who have laid the matter at the feet of the current president, Barack Obama, citing it as another example of Democratic "big brother" government run amok. It is Obama, they argue, who has fostered an atmosphere in which secret spying and shadowy government activity are not only allowed but also encouraged. Americans—yes, Republicans in particular—do seem to have short memories.

Oliver North… who's that? Dick Cheney? Don Rumsfeld? Never heard of 'em.

On September 16, 2001, just days following the attacks on the World Trade Center and Pentagon, the vice president of the United States, Richard "Dick" Cheney, sat with Tim Russert on *Meet the Press*. He said, "We'll have to work the dark side, if you will. We've got to spend time in the shadows… a lot of what needs to be done here will have to be done quietly, without any discussion, using sources and methods that are available." In the coming weeks, the Bush II administration would act. Things would happen quickly and without debate. Here, Cheney hinted at a policy of disregarding the Constitutional role of Congress as the voice of the people. The war on terror would be waged with decisions made by those few closest to the Oval Office.

Without any discussion. Those words should have sent shivers down the national spine. Members of both political parties—but Republicans especially, who have long raged against concentrated power—should have been alarmed. Why weren't they? Isn't it a matchless strength that this nation—made up of so many different religious and racial backgrounds—is able to debate difficult matters without resorting to violent outbursts (the 1960s notwithstanding)? Discussion is particularly American.

The vice president's words—and meaning—seemed to dovetail with thoughts once offered by a friend of mine who said, "Desperate times call for desperate measures." To play devil's advocate for a moment, let's assume that desperate times do—in fact—require desperate measures. What does that really mean? It means that anything goes. In other words, whatever it takes. If one really believes that sentiment, then it should surprise no one that the consequences of that belief often involve so-called extra-legal (or immoral) means.

In the Land of the Free though, such thinking is dangerous. Just how dangerous? An example I've used several times is this: that in 1901, one man—a disturbed man named Leon Czolgosz—took action that had giant repercussions. He was deeply troubled by what he saw as inequality in the United States, with men like J. P. Morgan and Andrew Carnegie having staggering wealth while others worked twelve-hour days in coal mines. Believing that such times called for desperate measures, Czolgosz shot and killed President William McKinley. I tend to shudder when I hear someone announce their belief that "desperate times call for desperate measures."

But this *is* what the vice president was saying. In 2001, I was not a foreign policy expert, nor had I ever served in the armed forces. I was only a college student at that time—attending the University of CT—yet I was immediately apprehensive when I watched Dick Cheney's interview on *Meet the Press*. It is entirely unfortunate that more Americans did not share my sense of doubt. Rather, most polls at that time expressed the public's mood to "kick some ass." They were with the VP. Someone had to pay for the awful events of September 11, and the American public was ready and willing to stand with a president—and his cabinet—who would (to stretch the VP's words) "work the dark side" and take us to war "without any discussion," using whatever "sources and methods" were available.

Despite the rhetoric of Mr. Cheney's statement, there was some discussion. More was needed, it was quickly determined, for US government agencies (the FBI, CIA, etc.) to—in a more effective way—actively engage in counterterrorism initiatives. Information gathering needed a boost; the process of information sharing between the different agencies needed updating. Knowing (in the aftermath) that men had entered the country with designs to carry out the September 11 attacks, holes in our border security needed to be addressed. What Congress came up with was a bipartisan bill, the Patriot Act, which was signed into law by President George W. Bush in October '01. The Patriot Act would allow law enforcement to more easily obtain warrants and wiretaps as well as business records during antiterrorism investigations; it also increased the penalties for those who commit crimes directly related to terrorist activity or for financially or materially assisting such activity. On paper this all sounded pretty good. Most honest Americans could support the idea that law enforcement need not have one arm tied behind its back while trying to catch criminals. But as with many good—even heroic—intentions, sometimes the law of unintended consequences has a way of sobering a free citizenry.

The Foreign Intelligence Surveillance Act of 1978 established a court—the FISA court—that would have the authority to either approve or deny warrants for information-gathering. During the Bush II administration, according to a December 15, 2005, James Risen article in the *New York Times*, eavesdropping activities were begun "without the court-approved warrants ordinarily required for domestic spying." Further in the article, it is maintained that senior White House officials asked that the article not be printed because its disclosures might jeopardize national security. The administration's main concern was not working with the FISA court or being open and transparent.

Much good was achieved because of the Patriot Act and because of efforts at state and local levels to help strengthen law enforcement, but there were also abuses (consider, for example, the Bush II team's dancing around the FISA court to approve *warrantless* wiretapping). Really, we should have seen it coming. Vice President Cheney said we would have to "spend time in the shadows." In the name of national security, officials would have an easier time listening in on conversations, of gathering information, of spying. And in the wake of the tragedy of September 11, people of both political parties nodded in agreement. *Okay, let's do this*. In order to better protect ourselves, we may have to give up a little personal privacy. *Okay*.

In his autobiography, called *In My Time* (published in 2011), Mr. Cheney discussed the NSA spying program. "Although parts of the NSA program remain classified," according to Cheney, "it is now public that a key element involved intercepting targeted communications into and out of the United States" (p. 349). He goes on to describe how, after the initial okay for the program was given, further examination would have to take place every thirty to forty-five days by the president and his staff. In March of 2004, in accordance with this aspect of the program, the VP held a congressional briefing, with such political heavyweights as Speaker of the House Denny Hastert

(R), Senate Majority Leader Bill Frist (R), House Minority Leader Nancy Pelosi (D), and Chairman of the House Select Committee on Intelligence Porter Goss (R). Vice President Cheney asked the group whether the program should continue, with the unanimous response that—yes—it should. He then asked if the administration should consider going before Congress to seek further approval to continue intelligence-gathering efforts. According to Mr. Cheney, "Again, the view around the table was unanimous. The members did not want us to seek additional legislation for the program. They feared, as did we, that going to the whole Congress would *compromise its secrecy*" (p. 351). I have added the italics here for emphasis.

Widespread domestic tapping of cell phones, monitoring of e-mails, using drones not only for spying but for military strikes—the foundation for these activities was laid with such decisions. And as noted, the aspect of secrecy was paramount. Those who today cry foul, who shout loud, long, and hard against such abuses of the public trust must have been either sleepwalking through the times or living under a rock while those in power passed the Patriot Act. They are—without question—attempting to rewrite history when they blame Barack Obama for giving birth to the abuses.

We are all in a way responsible for what took place in the halls of information-gathering agencies like the NSA. The cowboy attitude of "let's kick some ass and take names" was contagious in the aftermath of 9/11. (One may recall the lyrics of a Toby Keith song: "We'll put a boot in your ass, it's the American way.") That said, if an American president is to be blamed for fostering an atmosphere where big-government-style secret maneuverings were not only allowed but also encouraged, it is the forty-third—George W. Bush. That atmosphere was not *created by* but rather *passed along to* the current administration. It is now for President Obama—and all Americans—to deal with the fallout.

Make no mistake: just because the atmosphere of "whatever it takes" started and took root during the Bush II term does not excuse President Obama for continuing—or for not curtailing—practices that are abusive. If a child hits his friend and is caught in the act, it is not an acceptable excuse to say, "But he hit me first!" Can the current administration do more to protect the privacy of the American people? Absolutely. And it should.

CHAPTER TWELVE

What Scowcroft Said

This chapter will deal with the American decision—following 9/11—to make war with Iraq (or more specifically, with its leader, Saddam Hussein). I do not intend to cover the topic from every possible angle or for very many pages. There have been many books—some well researched and well written, others less so—about whether or not the United States (and her president) made the right call. Lots of ink has already been spilled in questioning the true nature of what drove the decision to invade Iraq (did we simply follow faulty intelligence, or was there an early, concerted effort to establish links that existed only in the most unreliable of reports?). I don't feel the need to revisit this well-worn path. (I may remind the reader, though, of the memo Donald Rumsfeld dictated on 9/11/2001—as described in chapter 10—in which he suggested going after "SH" as well as "UBL." With access to that bit of information in particular, the reader is here afforded free rein to consider the facts—and politics—of our common history and make up his/her own mind.) For those who are interested and have yet to delve into the labyrinth, I will suggest the following excellent books: *Hubris*, by Michael Isikoff and David Corn; *Rumsfeld: His Rise, Fall, and Catastrophic Legacy*, by Andrew Cockburn; *A Tragic Legacy*, by Glenn Greenwald; and *Why Presidents Fail*, by Richard M. Pious.

I will, to offer a balanced approach, also recommend reading the books *Decision Points*, by George W. Bush, and *In My Time*, by Dick Cheney.

I should note that *yes*, I have read each of the books listed. I found in them plenty of truly helpful material—offered from both sides of the divide—and have come away with a rich sense of being able to make reasoned judgments from an *informed* standpoint. Whatever conclusions a person may take away from studying the foreign policy decisions of the George W. Bush presidency—be they in accord with or in opposition to the president—I will suggest that the act itself (of studying, researching, thinking critically in the classroom sense of that term) is of terrific importance. To attempt a deeper understanding of the times we've recently lived through is, if nothing else, a constructive use of one's time. Such studies may—in time—provide us an opportunity to learn from our mistakes and keep us from repeating them.

* * *

"We know that Iraq and the Al Qaida terrorist network share a common enemy: the United States of America. We know that Iraq and Al Qaida have had high-level contacts that go back a decade. Some Al Qaida leaders who fled Afghanistan went to Iraq... and we know that after September the 11th, Saddam Hussein's regime gleefully celebrated the terrorist attacks on America."

President George W. Bush delivered those words in Cincinnati, Ohio, on October 7, 2002. It was an effort to put forth, in easily digested terms, his argument for American "intervention" in Iraq. His main point was that there was a concrete relationship between Saddam Hussein—the secular leader of a nation-state in the Middle East—and Al Qaida (the fundamentalist terrorist organization). In fact, one of the Al Qaida leaders he referenced in the speech (the "high-level contact") was Mohammed Atta, one of the 9/11 hijackers. According to Vice President Cheney (who repeated the charge not only during several appearances on *Meet the Press* but also in his autobiography, *In My Time*), Atta had—prior to the attacks—met with a senior Iraqi intelligence official in Prague.

"We came to a different conclusion," said John McLaughlin, who was deputy director of the CIA from 2000 to 2004. "We went over that every which way from Sunday. We looked at it from every conceivable angle. We peeled open the source and examined the 'chain of acquisition'; we looked at photographs; we looked at timetables." Former CIA officer Vincent Cannistraro, speaking during an interview for the PBS program *Frontline*, echoed McLaughlin's analysis. According to Cannistraro, "The FBI had Atta in Florida at the time." The CIA, then, seemed pretty firm in its belief that such a meeting did not take place (or at least that there was no credible evidence to indicate that it had).

But both the president and vice president continued to suggest that Atta met with Iraqi officials in Prague. Here it was—"Proof!" they professed, of an Al Qaida–Hussein relationship.

President Bush again addressed the supposed Iraqi threat in a speech given just a few months later, on March 17, 2003. This would be *the* speech. He listed reasons supporting his belief that Saddam Hussein posed a clear and present danger not only to neighboring countries in the Middle East but also to America. Aerial photographs, he said, had shown that efforts were underway in Iraq to produce dangerous chemical and biological weapons. Iraqi officials (including Saddam's sons) had threatened UN weapons inspectors. And they had—according to the president—supported Al Qaida terrorists.

Then the president offered an ultimatum:

> Saddam Hussein and his sons must leave Iraq within 48 hours. Their refusal to do so will result in military conflict, commenced at a time of our choosing. For their own safety, all foreign

nationals, including journalists and inspectors, should leave Iraq immediately.

(In other words, "Game on... your move.")

It was impossible to miss the deep conviction in his voice or the unyielding force of his words. There was a sense that it was high noon on a dust-covered patch of road in the Old West. For those who felt as strongly as President Bush did that Saddam was a real and unbending source of evil, the moment must have been electric. It was definitely reminiscent of Ronald Reagan's impassioned stand against Muammar Gaddafi in 1986 following the bombing of a Berlin discotheque. I was admittedly less certain of the true threat the Iraqi leader posed—at least to the United States (I hate to sound callous, but how he treated his own people didn't concern me)—and yet I, too, could feel the energy of the moment. One who is not active in the armed services can only imagine what those brave men and women were feeling.

It should be noted that in the months prior to the start of the war, we—the American public—had been assured and reassured by the administration that we (our forces) would be greeted by Iraqis as liberators. We all know what happened next. As I said, I feel no urgent need to revisit the entire history of the war. What follows, though, is important.

In a documentary on the life and presidency of George Herbert Walker Bush (the first President Bush) for the *American Experience* series on PBS, several of the president's friends / cabinet members discussed Desert Shield/Storm, America's first foray into Iraq. Our intervention, in January 1991, followed on the heels of Iraq's invasion of Kuwait—a country with friendly relations with the United States—and was viewed (at that time and over the years) as a positive affair. The United States (with support from a coalition of forces from other nations) set up a defensive line to ensure that Iraq would not invade Saudi Arabia. Following five weeks of chest-thumping intransigence, during which Saddam's military force remained—defiant and unmoving—in Kuwait, Congress approved the president's call to action. The US-led coalition pressed forward to drive Saddam's forces out. It was a quick, ultimately successful enterprise. Much of Saddam's military was crippled. Some Iraqis surrendered their weapons without ever having fired them.

President Bush chose to officially end the war after four days. (The ground offensive became known as the 100-hour war.) According to James A. Baker III (Bush's secretary of state), the war was concluded because "we... achieved what the UN Security Council resolution authorized us to do, that is: kick Iraq out of Kuwait." Saddam Hussein, though, remained in power.

Our objectives had been met. Bring the boys home. Colin Powell (chairman of the Joint Chiefs of Staff at that time) offered another important reason for the US decision to end hostilities with Saddam still in power. "We did not want to totally destroy the Iraqi army, and you can guess why: Iran." The comment is far-seeing. The two countries had a long and adversarial history which—if left alone—kept the Middle East (albeit uneasily) balanced. It was a shaky but workable sort of symmetry—the Middle Eastern model of stasis or equilibrium. "It was always our intention," Powell continued, "to leave Saddam Hussein with enough of an army... so that it would not leave him totally vulnerable to Iranian misadventure—keeping in mind that the Iraq-Iran War had only ended three years earlier."

A recollection from Brent Scowcroft—who was national security advisor for President Gerald Ford and for the first President Bush—helps support the combined assessments of Secretary Baker and General Powell.

It is worth a brief digression to describe General Scowcroft's bona fides. Even a cursory flip through his résumé is striking: one quickly recognizes Scowcroft as a man who—both in the military

(USAF) as well as in his private life—has dedicated himself to serving his country. After graduating from West Point in 1947, he earned a PhD in international relations from Columbia University. His career in the military—one that spanned twenty-nine years—included posts as professor of Russian history at West Point, head of political science at the Air Force Academy, and assistant air attaché in the US embassy in Belgrade, Yugoslavia. In 1972, he accepted a position as "military assistant" to President Richard Nixon; in 1975 (following Nixon's resignation in August '73) Scowcroft was reassigned, becoming President Ford's national security advisor.

General Scowcroft is a Republican; though (when one looks at his statements and positions over the years) it is apparent that he did not feel constrained to always tow the party line. This was due, perhaps, to the fact that he never ran for or held elective office. He was where he was—serving in each post—not out of party loyalty but because of a wish to serve. This, more than anything else, made his an important voice especially in the Bush I administration.

In the years following Desert Storm, many people proposed the question, Why did the United States choose *not* to remove Saddam Hussein from power in 1991 when we—clearly—had the opportunity to do so? The answer is here offered in clear prose: "We did not know," said General Scowcroft, "what would happen if we went on into Baghdad [the capital of Iraq]. It would have been simple to do. But we would've been occupiers in a hostile land... and we had no exit plan. How do you get out once you've occupied the country?"

A chill may be felt prickling at the back of the reader's neck as he or she reads General Scowcroft's thoughts, especially that last haunting sentence: *how do you get out once you've occupied the country?* If Saddam were to be ousted, someone would need to remain as an occupying force to impose stability. As we've seen, in Saddam's Hussein's absence—or when a power vacuum opened up—the remaining opposing forces (in this case Sunni and Shia, whose differences are political rather than spiritual) would wrestle for the opportunity to fill the void. The price paid for attempting to remove the dictator—a foolish venture with little consideration given to planning an exit strategy—would be realized during the Bush II presidency. The national dialogue would, under W's watch, involve terms such as *insurgents* and *road-side bombing*.

It is altogether appropriate to repeat a rhetorical question made in an earlier chapter (chapter 4) when examining the country's strategic goals: does the foreign policy offer structure to a weak and hurting global community? Let's attempt a literal application of that particular thought process with a question that is not at all rhetorical: did the foreign policy objectives of the Bush II administration make the United States in particular (and the world in general) more safe? I would contend that for any educated person, the answer is clear. W's legacy, in terms of foreign policy, is—much like Ronald Reagan's—agonizing to consider.

In the years following Saddam Hussein's ouster—as evidence of either (1) Colin Powell's psychic abilities as a fortune-teller or (2) his ability to think strategically—Iran has indeed emerged as a bellicose voice thundering from the Middle East. Perhaps General Scowcroft was also psychic. His personal remembrances conclude—for the purposes of this chapter—with this, a rejoinder to those voices that questioned the wisdom of decisions made by our government in 1991. "For a number of years we heard 'Why didn't you finish the job'. We don't hear that anymore."

It is a tragedy of global scale that George W. Bush (the forty-third president) did not have the same cautious men in his corner (particularly Baker and Scowcroft) that his father, the forty-first president, had. One again wonders, what if?

CHAPTER THIRTEEN

Now, Be Nice

It was—I think—fifteen years ago that my maternal grandma made me a box. It was for memories, jewelry (at that time, as a "cool dude" in the late 1990s, I had my ear pierced), photos, and whatever other important things that an organized pack rat might want to keep. I lived for a year (2003–04) in Georgia, and—yes—the box made both trips (there and home again) with me. In it, I've kept letters, little notes, and pictures: small things that—while they mean something to me—might be of little interest to anyone else. In 2010, I added Grandma's funeral card to the collection of personal memories I keep in the box.

There is a piece of paper that is among the items I've kept in the box, a single sheet from the voter registration office. It is dated September 11, 2009. It is the paperwork officially recognizing a change made in party affiliation. In the years before that date, I was a Republican. The change had been a long time coming: in 2000 I voted the Republican ticket during the presidential election; however, in 2004 and again in 2008, I was a Republican who voted for the Democratic ticket. At that time, I tried to discuss my reasons with a friend, and I recall telling him that I hadn't left the party—it left me. I wasn't trying to be cute. I meant what I said. I still stand behind that statement.

In the twenty-five years since Ronald Reagan sat in the Oval Office, the Republican Party has changed in ways that would make Reagan's conservative predecessors—Barry Goldwater comes to mind—fail to recognize it. Even Reagan would, I think, be impressed with just how much it has changed. I will make the argument—successfully, I hope—that the changes have not been for the better. One *especially* significant change has taken place: a breakdown in civility and in political willingness to find (or even discuss) compromise.

Once upon a time, politicians of opposite parties found ways to constructively deal with one another. There are far too many examples to go through them all; however, because this *is* chapter 13, I might cite Millard Fillmore (the thirteenth president of the United States). Fillmore was the second so-called accidental president (a Buffalo politician who—as VP—rose to the presidency following the death of Zachary Taylor), and he is one of the largely forgotten presidents. His term of office is remembered for one thing: the Compromise of 1850.

The United States had gained vast amounts of territory as a result of the Mexican War. The question of whether this new land would enter the union as free or slave was at the heart of rising tensions. It was a terribly difficult time, with Northern abolitionists and Southern "gentlemen" looking to Washington in hopes of settling the matter. (Of course there were those on both sides of the argument who were perfectly willing to settle things with fists and bullets.) Henry Clay—the old Kentucky politician—managed to fashion a "compromise bill," which contained certain measures that would satisfy the North as well as provisions (such as an extension of the Fugitive Slave Law) that would please the South, but it looked as though the bill was getting nowhere in Congress. In fact, President Taylor suggested that if the bill did find its way to his desk, he would veto it.

Enter Millard Fillmore. When he became president, he could easily have done nothing and allowed the compromise bill to die in Congress. Certainly, there were those who suggested it would be foolish for Fillmore to take any course that opposed the policies Taylor embraced before his death. Fillmore chose to act: he endorsed the bill. The Compromise of 1850 was not a perfect solution, and of course, it did not resolve the problems that eventually led the nation to Civil War—but it did offer a temporary release of the building tensions. Had the Compromise not been approved—with President Fillmore's support—it is possible that the Civil War could have sparked a full decade sooner than it did.

At that crucial moment in American history, both Henry Clay and Millard Fillmore appreciated the importance of compromise. Their efforts weren't perfect, but they were—I believe—necessary. In their own time (the 1980s), Ronald Reagan (R) and Tip O'Neill (D) worked to find compromise positions. In the last twenty-five years, though, especially in Republican circles, the very word—*compromise*—has become a sort of four-letter word. One who does not embrace the party line 100 percent—or worse, who works with others across the aisle—is considered a kind of renegade or prodigal son and is fair game: open, in other words, to disapproval and to possible primary challenges from true believers. (As this chapter is being written, in fact, Senator Mitch McConnell is preparing for a 2014 midterm in which he is being challenged not by a "bleeding heart" liberal looking to unseat him, but by Matt Bevin, who charges that Mr. McConnell is not "conservative enough." In realistic terms, to call McConnell anything other than conservative is laughable—unless you are of the Bevin wing of the party.)

This is an attitude that leads—as we have seen—to dysfunctional government.

Rather than sort through and try to find points of agreement, Republican leaders in Washington today seem prepared—eager, even—to embrace an all-or-nothing mind-set. Too often, now, we hear ugly utterances. Those who have a different point of view and who disagree with President Obama (Tea Partiers, for example) show no real interest in compromise; rather, they have time and again called the president "un-American." This simplistic, black-and-white view of the world is troubling. It holds that "you're either with me or against me," "you either agree with *my* vision of how America should behave, or you are 'un-American.'" This is a mind-set that does not easily allow for compromise, creating instead an environment where even the word *moderate* has also fallen into disrepute. People who have adopted this mind-set forget that John Adams and Thomas Jefferson (who fought together for independence) had wildly different visions for what America should be. (They had many of the same arguments, in fact, that we continue to have today.) And both were, in the very best definition of the term, American.

Leaders who are unwilling to engage in a search for common ground—of compromising—close themselves to the possibility not because they are (at heart) bad people but because they believe doing so is a disgraceful giving-up of one's ideals. These people offer little in the way of genuine leadership. Had such people been in charge in 1850, the Civil War *definitely* would have begun a decade sooner. Thank God we had Millard Fillmore.

I have had friendly disagreements with coworkers while discussing one political issue or another. In previous chapters, I've provided examples of our lunchtime exchanges. Sometimes we've agreed, at other times, not so much. I have never once suggested (and hope I never will) that because of our differences, the other person is "un-American." Most behavior is learned. In responsible homes, we are taught to tie our shoes; we are taught to share our toys; we are taught not to lie. I was taught to be respectful of others. In other ways and in meaner homes, we are taught ugliness. (No child is born ready to use the n-word or call another child "un-American.") Neither party should adopt nastiness as a part of its dialogue.

And yet, it cannot be ignored that lately one party has done exactly that. Though George W. Bush was not the first president to paint opposition forces with a wide, accusing brush, the current (very heated) temperature of the dialogue in DC can be traced to (and certainly took root during) the Bush II presidency. After 9/11 and for the rest of his term, Bush argued that those who disagreed with the White House—especially in regards to foreign policy and national security decisions—were acting irresponsibly, potentially putting the United States in danger. Administration officials (including VP Cheney) backed up this rhetoric, suggesting that those who opposed US intervention in Iraq, for example, were acting against the national interest. (There it was, for all to see, that distorted way of thinking that says "You're either with us or against us.") In the 2004 presidential race, in fact, the president ran a campaign that—in a very direct way—said, basically, "Vote for me because I've kept you safe" (the understanding, of course, being that a vote for the other guy—John Kerry—would be a potentially dangerous choice).

It is clear that airing such toxic implications helps support the creation and maintenance of a divided, even bitter relationship between the parties. So much for being a "uniter, not a divider."

Just as the last pages of this text were being written, a news story broke that directly related to this chapter's subject matter. In January, rock musician Ted Nugent (who, following the Sandy Hook tragedy when the country was busy debating gun control, said that President Obama should "suck on [his] machine gun") appeared at a gun trade show and was quoted as calling the president a "subhuman mongrel." To be fair, one cannot truthfully admit to being surprised by Nugent's language (he's not exactly known for diplomacy). But the rank atmosphere in which such language often goes unchallenged—in which one cannot agree to disagree and where simple disagreement becomes an open arena for such disgusting bigotry—has (sadly) become rather commonplace. The problem, in fact, was not that Nugent said what he did, but that Greg Abbott (the Republican front-runner in this year's Texas gubernatorial race)—or, more likely someone on Abbott's staff—scheduled two campaign appearances with the musician. To offer Ted Nugent (a person who has—time and again—offered such distasteful, offensive thoughts) part of the spotlight during an important political race was either (1) an exercise in extremely poor judgment or (2) a revealing moment in which the candidate's own political insensitivity was highlighted. An Internet search within the last few days exposes the degree to which nastiness has taken root in our political landscape: sites have sprung up supporting "Ted Nugent for president."

To their lasting credit, some Republicans (including both Rand Paul and John McCain) have openly voiced disgust and disapproval for Nugent's statement, saying—as I have above—that such nastiness does not belong in the national political dialogue. There are others in the GOP though (Michelle Bachmann comes to mind, as does Rush Limbaugh) who can rightly take credit for fostering this ugly atmosphere with their own abusive language. I repeat the sentiment expressed above: that in responsible homes, we are taught respect for others; in other ways and in meaner homes, we are taught ugliness. One wonders—and may easily guess—from which of these two environments people like Nugent and Limbaugh spring.

If it wishes to regroup from the recent losses (the presidential races in 2008 and 2012) and do something to help itself in future contests, the Republican Party should consider shedding the uglier, fringe elements that it has lately embraced. Step 1: The Tea Party should be removed from Republican ranks and allowed to exist on its own as a legitimate third party. While it does share some basic principles with traditional Republican orthodoxy, the Tea Party is much more antigovernment than the GOP has *ever* been. Can you imagine, for example, President Dwight Eisenhower (a Republican who presided over the construction of the Interstate Highway system) suggesting—and cheering for—a government shutdown? Of course not.

Step 2: Take a stand. Do as my father's mother (my paternal grandma) suggested when she said, "Now, be nice." Members of the GOP (certainly its leaders) should follow the honorable example and do what Senators Rand Paul and John McCain recently did: denounce—*loudly* denounce—men and women who show up to local town hall meetings and call President Obama "evil" and "un-American" (or worse). Refuse to share space on the public stage alongside people like Ted Nugent. Remind audiences at public rallies, those dedicated voters, of the extraordinary line in Thomas Jefferson's first inaugural address: "We are all Republicans, we are all Federalists." In other words, we—liberals and conservatives alike—are all Americans.

While it was definitely a principal factor, this trend toward divisive ugliness was not the only thing that spurred my leaving the Republican fold. Much of what this book deals with—the central focus of my efforts, in other words—is the ongoing problem of hypocrisy. It is easy to provide examples: a personal favorite is Ronald Reagan calling for less government spending, all the while spending unconscionable sums—and creating huge deficits—in order to finance his arms race with Russia (as discussed in chapter 3). I do not mean to suggest that any one party has a monopoly in this respect; however, it has been this writer's experience that the GOP has—in recent years—done a remarkable job in diligently proclaiming one thing while practicing another. While one can easily devote enormous stacks of paper—bookshelves, even—to the topic, I will attempt a brief analysis in the next chapter.

CHAPTER FOURTEEN

God and the Republican Party

"He was in many respects a 'senator's senator'. He could differ but he was never personal, he was never vindictive. He had enormously powerful conservative beliefs about freedom." The quote is from Senator Edward M. Kennedy, wherein he describes a longtime Republican colleague—Barry M. Goldwater, of Arizona.

In fact, Barry Goldwater and Teddy's brother Jack were good friends. "He's the kind of antagonist that I've always enjoyed," Goldwater said of JFK. "I imagine that I've debated the President more on the floor of the Senate than any other man, and it never affected our friendship." (I could have used these quotes in chapter 13 as strong examples of how cordial politics used to be.)

In my years as a Republican, I considered myself a Reagan Republican. In retrospect, however, it seems I was very much a Goldwater Republican. Barry Goldwater was an American original (and is often referred to as "Mr. Conservative" for his role in fathering the conservative movement in the GOP). His conservatism was honest and deeply felt. And of the many titles he wore—air force pilot during WWII, five-term US Senator from Arizona (retiring in 1987), Republican presidential candidate (1964), husband, father, amateur radio enthusiast—there was one thing he was not: a hypocrite. When Mr. Goldwater called for smaller government, he meant exactly that—smaller, less involved, less authoritarian. His vision was for a government that was unconcerned with delving into an individual's private affairs, unwilling to entangle itself in the business of telling people how to live their lives (that is to say, a truly conservative government). This was the shared vision of the Republican Party.

Was being the operative word.

Sadly, in the last twenty-five years, Republicans have collectively turned their backs on genuine (dare I say Goldwater-style) conservatism and have instead embraced the politics of hypocrisy. In fact, a strong argument can be made—and I will so argue—that things have changed so dramatically within the party that the GOP that Barry Goldwater championed no longer exists.

The greatest example of Republican hypocrisy—the one that ultimately forced me to reexamine my politics and change party affiliation—involves that continued call for a less intrusive government. This has long been a concept that is foundational to the party's vision for American government, predating Barry Goldwater. And it is an *honest* point of view. Even following my conversion as a Democrat, there are still aspects of thinking that recall my earlier politics. (For example, I firmly believe that the decision of whether or not to allow smoking in a particular venue—say, a restaurant or bar—should rest with the owner of the establishment and not with government. We—as free citizens—then have the right and can choose whether or not we wish to patronize that establishment.) Barry would applaud this train of thought.

The hypocrisy arrives, however, when the reasonable call for less intrusion collides with Republican stands on certain issues (those that we breezily call the "social issues"): health care, marriage equality, and abortion, to name a few. The pressing question is this: Why has the Republican Party adopted certain strident—seemingly immovable—

positions that are in *direct* contravention with the fundamental call for a smaller, less intrusive government? (An entire book—or series of books—can be dedicated to exploring this important problem.) The answer is a rather troubling one. It involves what can—in my mind—best be described as the GOP's unhealthy relationship with (and the concentrated effort to court) the evangelical vote.

Religion and politics have had a long and difficult history in our country. I will offer one poignant example that colorfully illustrates the tension between the two worlds. It involved a presidential race:

In 1928, Democratic candidate Al Smith lost the presidential election to Republican Herbert Hoover in a landslide. Much of the outcome rested with Hoover's popularity; however, another—very key—aspect to which Smith owed his loss was his Catholicism. He was, in fact, the first Catholic to win a party's nomination for the presidency. There was a wide fear that if Smith won, the government would be greatly influenced by the pope. This may not have been a fair assessment of Smith or of his inclinations, but it is what happened. Such concerns resurfaced in 1960 when John F. Kennedy ran against Richard Nixon. (In this case, of course, Kennedy's religion did not have the same determinative ill effects that Smith experienced.)

The fear that so capsized Al Smith's run for the presidency harkens back to a long-established concern in American governance: the separation of church and state. It is a fear that seems all but erased from the minds of today's elected leaders.

Whereas the belief in less intrusive government *should* lead the party to reject involving itself in personal matters that are best left between a man or woman and his/her pastor, for example, we have seen in the last twenty-odd years the exact opposite occur. If a congregation is willing to allow same-sex marriages, it should be left to that particular group to do so without legislators stepping in. If a vote is held (with "we the people" speaking their minds through ballot) and a state decides to recognize such marriages, Republican representatives in the state—not to mention those of other states—should have nothing at all to say in the matter. That is, they should have nothing to say—if they are *true believers* in "limited government." This is true (Goldwater) conservatism.

In recent months, we have seen a raucous Republican outcry in opposition to the Affordable Care Act (ObamaCare), suggesting that the law is an obtrusive example of overreaching "big-government." The cry is easily recognized: how dare the federal government assume such heavy-handed authority over a free people and their medical choices! How despotic! (So the thinking goes.) This is, of course, a *perfectly legitimate* view and is in accord with the foundational argument for small, less involved government. Let's apply that very thinking, though, to a related issue now being widely debated. Somehow—almost unbelievably—Republican lawmakers seem unable (perhaps unwilling?) to connect the dots.

If a woman seeks an abortion—let's for a moment leave aside the distracting arguments over *why* the procedure is being sought—true Republican belief in smaller government should regard the decision as a personal one best left between the patient and her doctor. A 1972 opinion written by Supreme Court Justice William J. Brennan (who was appointed to the court by Dwight Eisenhower) says, "If the right of privacy means anything it is the right of the individual, married or single, to be free from unwarranted governmental intrusion into matters so fundamentally affecting a person as the decision whether to bear or beget a child." We don't want the government making our medical choices (right?). Wrong. Apparently, the Republican Party sees no problem with inconsistent thinking (railing against excessive government intrusion under ObamaCare while—in the very same breath—meddling legislatively in the most personal, private moments of a woman's life). In the last several years, there have been many antiabortion bills (at local and state levels)—some successfully passed, others stalled—that seek to restrict the ability to obtain the procedure. They all have one thing in common: each has been introduced by so-called conservative legislators and enjoy wide Republican support.

Voters of both parties should call more attention to this hypocritical nonsense. It is this "split personality" kind of hypocrisy (of calling for smaller government while simultaneously proposing *more* government interposition in our private affairs) that likely has Senator Barry Goldwater—who passed away in 1998—tossing Heaven's chairs around in frustration. John Dean (the one-time White House counsel to Richard Nixon), who authored several books, including *Broken Government* and a book detailing the senator's displeasure with the extreme right called *Pure Goldwater*, was a Goldwater family friend. Mr. Dean's recollections do suggest that the hypocrisy I've detailed here would indeed ruffle the man we still call Mr. Conservative.

According to Dean, "He [Goldwater] thought that they had no business being in areas like abortion and sex. One thing after another, he just was appalled that this had become sort of the growing… concern of the Republican party."

The new GOP vision, in fact, does seem to be for smaller government for those who agree with specific Evangelical thoughts; for everyone else, proposals are offered, which say that "we'll be there to tell you what—and what *not*—to do in the bedroom and/or doctor's office." The new definition, then, of *small government* would seem to be "a government that taxes less but that sneaks a peek in the window to make sure you're being a 'good Catholic.'"

What is the root cause of such disjointed thinking? As suggested above, the answer lies in the Republican embrace of evangelical thought. The GOP has, in a rather transparent manner, turned away from the American belief in freedom of religion in order to win the Southern Baptist vote. Men like Mike Huckabee (who was himself an ordained minister before becoming governor of Arkansas in 1996) have polluted the political environment in Washington with a particularly divisive form of leadership. Freedom of religion means exactly that—freedom. While there are certainly secular laws that conform to religious norms (thou shall not steal), no one belief system is supposed to be able to impose its rules on the whole of our society. "We the people" are not all followers of one religion. Our politics cannot—should not—be swayed by religious arguments.

And yet this is exactly what we have allowed in Republican discussions. The emotional debate on abortion is consistently—and heavily—sprinkled with religious reasons for opposing the practice. People who attend public pro-life rallies can often be seen carrying signs that read "God is for life" and "Babies are angels." I believe there *are* honest reasons for adopting a pro-life point of view. In a free society, reasonable men and women with good hearts are able to come to different political conclusions. That said, the injection of religion into the discussion is (I must go against my earlier objections and call this for what it is) un-American. In this case, the term is justified.

When, in the 1980s, Barry Goldwater felt it necessary to stand up to the likes of commentator/ televangelist Jerry Falwell, he had this to say: "If it's gonna take a fight, they're gonna find ol' Goldy fighting like hell. I'm probably the most conservative member of Congress, and I don't like to get kicked around by people who call themselves conservative on a non-conservative matter." When Falwell was quoted on the record as saying that "good Christians should oppose" the nomination of Goldwater's fellow Arizonan Sandra Day O'Connor to the Supreme Court, Barry said in response, "All good Christians should kick him [Falwell] in the ass."

Goldwater was appropriately gutsy—even feisty— in his assertions. He said, "I came to this Congress thirty years ago opposing the concentration of power in the hands of unions. And I have to oppose it today in the hands of church groups." Well said, Mr. Goldwater.

He continued to pounce: "Ol' Tom Jefferson had us separate the church and state, and the 'religious right' scares the hell outta me. They have no place in politics." He was right. It is true: the Founding Fathers of this great country (Washington, Adams, Jefferson, and company) were men who *did* believe in a higher authority. But they also believed in our own unique capacity as free men/women—as Americans—to make important decisions *without* forcing any particular set of religious beliefs upon one another. Legislation was not—and should not be—a matter of religious faith.

The grave marker for Thomas Jefferson, the father of conservative thought, notes his authorship of the Virginia Statute for Religious Freedom (to which Goldwater's last statement refers). Jefferson's close friend and advisor James Madison, in a letter dated July 10, 1822, said of the United States: "We are teaching the world the great truth that governments do better without kings and nobles than with them. The merit will be doubled by the other lesson that religion flourishes in greater purity without than with the aid of government."

Amen.

And there is this: "Congress shall make no law respecting an establishment of religion, or prohibiting the free exercise thereof." These are the first sixteen words in the First Amendment to the Constitution. (Somebody may want to give Mike Huckabee a copy.) As laws are applied to *all* Americans, they cannot be made to suit the specific religious beliefs of a few. Though we as a nation may not wish to (nor should we) return to the unjustified fear that overturned Al Smith's candidacy in 1928, we should regard religious language in political debates with a dedicated American sense of distrust.

In chapter 8, mention was made (while examining an excerpt of his first inaugural address) of George W. Bush's religious faith. I will repeat here what was previously said: that his faith is genuine and is one of the best parts of his character. Let me be absolutely crystal clear. Though I was raised Catholic and have—since adulthood—moved away from the practice of that faith, I do not take issue with or question anyone's religious devotion. At issue is *not*, do George W. Bush and Mike Huckabee really believe? They do. (Neither is the question, should believers hold elective office? John Kennedy answered that particular concern nicely.) The issue is, as discussed, the use of personal faith in deciding political matters.

Those who today call themselves conservative—who argue for smaller government while proposing intrusive legislation—are really anything but. They've created in the GOP a hypocritical tendency and in doing so have terribly distorted the conservative movement that Barry M. Goldwater helped create. They also caused some young Republicans like me to abandon ship.

From January of 2001 to January 2009, during the turbulent years of the George W. Bush administration, those church groups of the religious right (that "scared the hell outta" Goldwater) had a very good friend in the Oval Office, and the invisible line separating church and state became very thin, indeed.

CHAPTER FIFTEEN

Terri Schiavo

On February 25, 1990, a twenty-seven-year-old woman named Terri Schiavo collapsed in her Florida home. After two months in the hospital, during which time she lay in a coma, her condition was updated to that of "persistent vegetative state." For several years, doctors worked in hopes of returning Terri to a responsive state; their efforts, however, were unsuccessful. In 1998, realizing that speech and physical therapy efforts had failed to make any gain or to improve her condition, Terri's husband Michael petitioned the court (as her legal guardian) to have Terri's feeding tube removed. He believed Terri would not want to continue to linger in such a state.

Terri's parents, Robert and Mary Schindler, opposed the move. They suggested that (as a Roman Catholic) Terri would not wish to defy church teachings on suicide. The removal of her feeding tube would, according to Terri's parents, bear little difference to a distraught person choosing to end his or her life with a self-inflicted gunshot wound. The problem for the court—beyond the matter of an internal family disagreement—was this: that Terri (who, at twenty-seven years old and in relatively fine health) did not have a living will that would disclose her end-of-life wishes.

The lack of a will necessitated a trial to determine what Terri's wishes might have been regarding life-prolonging measures. The trial judge—citing the claim that reliable oral disclosures between husband and wife had occurred (and that such disclosures would buttress his wishes)—initially ruled in Michael Schiavo's favor and approved the petition.

This decision was followed by years of dramatic court appearances, videotapes, and subsequent appeals by the Schindlers, an appeal to overturn Michael Schiavo's relationship as Terri's legal guardian (denied), to allow the Schindlers to attempt natural feeding with the patient (denied), and a second appeal that would allow her parents to attempt to feed Terri by mouth (denied). When her parents' final appeal was exhausted, Republicans in the Florida legislature passed Terri's Law, which allowed then governor Jeb Bush the authority to intervene. (As discussed in the previous chapter, true Republican orthodoxy—the belief in limited, less intrusive government—would have forced Governor Bush to *reject* intervention. He did not.) Further appeals were now brought before the court in which the question of the constitutionality of Terri's Law was deliberated. (The law was eventually found to be unconstitutional.)

President George W. Bush—a born again Christian (not to mention brother of the governor of Florida)—and congressional Republicans then intervened, passing a bill proposed by Senator Rick Santorum (R), which transferred jurisdiction of the Schiavo case from Florida state courts to federal courts. In a move that must have frustrated the president, federal courts refused to overrule the state court decisions. Terri Schiavo, whose tragic circumstances had garnered first state and then national attention, died March 31, 2005.

It is incredible—that is, it is incredible to any reasonable mind—to consider what happened in this case: to think of the lengths to which state legislators, the (Republican!) governor of Florida, and the (Republican!) president of the United States went in order to involve themselves in what was a private legal dispute. The greater issues of right to life, legal guardianship, right to death (as in a person's consenting to DNR instructions in a living will), and religious beliefs and practices all created a storm that certain politicians were unable to resist engaging.

One may imagine the ghost of Barry Goldwater shaking his head in disbelief.

On March 27, 2014 (according to the website www.terrisfight.org), the Life & Hope Network—formerly the Terri Schindler Schiavo Foundation—will hold an award gala with "honored speaker" Glenn Beck. Individual tickets to the event will set back interested persons $150. (For those who have deep pockets, there are also sponsorship opportunities from $100 to $12,500.) In 2013, the "honored speaker" was Sarah Palin, the one-time Republican vice-presidential hopeful. Under a banner that reads "Our Mission," visitors to the website will discover that the Life & Hope Network is a nonprofit organization whose mission is to "build a network of support" for what it calls the "medically dependent" (people in a vegetative state) and their families. It is an organization made up of people—honest people—who call for the preservation of life, even when the life in question is one reduced to feeding tubes and mechanisms that perform the function of breathing for the patient.

One imagines that those in charge of the daily operations of the Life & Hope Network (L&HN) were very excited to get such notable political personalities to speak at the events in 2013 and '14. Sarah Palin in particular is well-known for her vocal pro-life advocacy. As a presidential candidate in 2012, while speaking with CBS news anchor Katie Couric, Palin said, "I am pro-life, and I am unapologetic in my position that I am pro-life." She confirmed that she was against abortion in any case, even for pregnancies that were the unhappy outcome of rape. "I would counsel to choose life, and persuade them [rape victims] to choose life for their babies." Her outspoken belief in the sanctity of life easily fits—hand in glove, so-to-speak—with the life-sustaining mission of the L&HN. Life is precious and therefore should not be tossed away in its earliest stages (abortion) or in its later, tragic hours (see the Schiavo case).

(It may be worthwhile to remind readers that Palin is a Republican who is unfalteringly against government interposition in our lives.)

The Republican position has thus become terrifically cloudy: a desire for smaller government, coupled with an intense, almost—you'll pardon the pun—religious desire to instruct the rest of us ("We the people") on how to live, procreate, and die.

Wait. It gets better.

Sarah Palin and Glenn Beck both support capital punishment. That's right: they have spoken *in favor* of the death penalty (she as the former governor of Alaska and failed political candidate, he as a "conservative" radio/television personality). So much for being "unapologetically pro-life."

Hypocrisy abounds.

CHAPTER SIXTEEN

A Painful Legacy
(or Afternoon in America?)

When Ulysses S. Grant left the White House in 1877, he left behind a lasting legacy (tarnished, though it was, by scandals not of his own design) of successful nation rebuilding. He is today remembered less for the scandals of his administration and more for his efforts to secure the rights and safety of the former slaves. It was Grant's leadership not *during* but *after* the Civil War that brought the wounded country back together. He was a man of war—who had at one time been called a butcher—whose parting gift to the nation was a ringing phrase that was immortalized on his tomb: "Let us have peace."

To borrow a modern phrase, Grant was "a uniter, not a divider."

Though I am (through personal temperament) of the isolationist bent, I admit to being awed by the words and deeds Woodrow Wilson offered his country in terms of an inheritance: a legacy of defending humanity from barbarism. On April 2, 1917, Wilson addressed Congress, asking for a declaration of war against Germany. He said, "The world must be made safe for democracy."

Wilson's legacy was not the peace that Grant had wished for America, but with his vision for a League of Nations, he hoped that one day the United States and other countries would all find a way *toward* peace. For better (and oftentimes for worse), we have been living with the ghost of Woodrow Wilson—and internationalism—ever since.

George W. Bush's presidency came to an end January 20, 2009. As previously noted, his was an important tenure. It was also a very controversial one, with striking repercussions that will be felt—at home and abroad—for a long time to come. Whatever one might think of the *man*, it would be rather difficult for anyone to suggest that George W. Bush's legacy is a positive one. Though he came into office wanting to extend hope and unity (to be a uniter), he left in his wake anger and division.

He also left behind a bigger government. Following the events of September 11, 2001, the "smaller is better" Republican president created the Department of Homeland Security. A new, heavy-handed bureaucracy was added to the functions of the federal government. The next time a Republican legislator is forced to remove his shoes and undergo a full-body scan at the airport before he can enjoy the uncomfortable seats and other pleasures of air travel—and who is (to complete the picture) all the while bemoaning the evils of "big brother" democratic government—he may wish to take a moment's time of honest reflection and thank George W. Bush for the experience.

The next time that same imaginary Republican traveler laments the awful abuses of privacy through government wire-tapping and domestic spying (once again, in a moment of honest reflection), he knows whom he should rightfully thank.

"Yes," some say, "Bush made the federal government bigger, but that was in response to the horrible terrorist attacks. He had to! And anyway, think of what he did for the American people through his tax cuts!" Okay, let's.

Republicans have long derided Democrats as tax-and-spend politicians who endanger America's economic health through such activity. (Never mind that in 1993, President Bill Clinton signed the

Omnibus Budget Reconciliation Act—it passed Congress without Republican support—which cut taxes for 15 million low-income families and small businesses.) When George W. Bush took office in 2001, part of his agenda was his goal to give Americans a tax cut. Sounds good, right? I can't think of anyone—myself included—who would turn his nose up to keeping more of his/her earned income in pocket. The economy was doing well, after all. It could take it. Before what became known as the Bush tax cuts, the highest marginal income tax rate (ITR) was somewhere around 39 percent. After the cuts, the highest ITR was 35 percent.

In a relatively stable economy—that is to say, in "good times"—such cuts are welcomed. When the country sets itself on a war footing, however (as it did after 9/11), one is forced to reevaluate the situation. War is an expensive endeavor, both in terms of human initiative/sacrifice and in financial (or pocketbook) engagement. President Bush, as discussed in earlier chapters, led the nation into a "war on terror," which was at first launched in the hills of Afghanistan and then proceeded into Iraq. The tax cuts remained in place. This meant that the United States generally (and her government specifically) had less revenue with which to pay for the war. Greater spending *without* the necessary revenue to cover the costs—this was Mr. Bush's "gift" to the American economy.

Richard N. Haass was director of policy planning in the Department of State under George W. Bush. In his excellent book *Foreign Policy Begins at Home: The Case for Putting America's House in Order*, he says, "George W. Bush fought costly wars in Iraq and in Afghanistan, allowed discretionary domestic spending to increase at an annual rate of 6 percent, and cut taxes deeply. The fiscal position of the United States declined in eight years from a surplus of just over $100 billion in 2001… to an estimated deficit of approximately $1.4 trillion in 2009" (p. 29). According to Haass, this led the cumulative federal debt to increase "from just under $6 trillion in 2001 to $10 trillion over that same period" (p. 29).

I contend that such an irresponsible economic record is rather reminiscent of Ronald Reagan's time in office.

You're thinking "Holy crap!" right? Indeed. Rather than a burst of conservative Republican outrage, however, there was—throughout the eight years of the Bush II administration—a surge in flag-waving patriotic display. Any person in the political world—local, state, or national—found second-guessing the administration (or without a flag pin on his/her lapel!) was immediately suspect. "Don't you support the war? Aren't you an American?" As for conservative thoughts about the economic dangers of deficit spending, these went by the wayside, only to find new life and new breath when Barack Obama became president.

This, then, was the Bush economic legacy. What of other domestic affairs?

As discussed, the government—far from having less of a role in our private lives—exercised greater interposition. For those who will argue this point, I will refer you to chapter 15 and the struggles of the Schiavo family.

If you were a person of faith, perhaps you didn't mind the government's new intrusive role during the Bush years. The first time Mr. Bush used his veto power as president involved a bill allocating government funding for stem-cell research. It is evident that his personal religious beliefs drove this action; this is understandable generally (church/state having received attention and analysis in chapter 14) because stem-cell research as a specific issue has wide room for disagreements, religious *or otherwise*. An honest person can believe that the destruction of an embryo for any reason would constitute the ending of a life, regardless of faith. Once again, however, there exists an example of deep hypocrisy:

"I was the governor of a state that had the death penalty and, as far as I was concerned, I reviewed every case and was confident that every person that had been put to death received full rights and was guilty of the crime charged." The quote is from—you guessed it—George W. Bush. He strongly favors the death penalty (as governor of Texas, he oversaw the executions of 152 souls). To be clear, at one point in time, Mr. Bush, each of those 152 people was an embryo.

His was a disappointing legacy in economic terms, and let's call it confused in domestic policy (contradictorily calling for smaller government while creating a new bureaucracy and plenty of red tape to accompany it, standing up for the unborn—through use of the presidential veto no less—while simultaneously supporting capital punishment, etc.). I don't wish to sound hyperpartisan or mean-spirited, but I must admit to having a difficult time not imagining circus music playing when I imagine what it's like to set up camp in Bush's brain: a place where such inconsistent public stands make sense.

What of foreign policy? This is where the Bush legacy suffers greatest (and where we—as Americans—will, for a long time, live with the consequences).

This chapter began by briefly reflecting on the ghosts of Grant and Wilson. It is Wilson's ghost in particular that has given the United States much to worry about. Isolationism gained a measure of support after WWI (it certainly gave its last foundering breath after WWII), and it can be argued that since Wilson's time in office, the United States has been concretely on an internationalist path. We are—and have been, despite the shared visions of Washington, Adams, Jefferson, etc.—engaged (one may use the Founders' term *entangled*) with the rest of the world. For better or worse, it is wishful thinking to hope that this nation could return to Warren Harding's "normalcy" of a more isolated course (let's worry about our own problems/affairs and let others deal with theirs). We are left, rather, to try our best to navigate global waters while suffering—or causing others to suffer—the least amount of disruption or ill effect. At this we have a patchy, checkered record at best.

Especially in the Middle East.

Without returning to the subject of already written chapters, we can here note simply that George W. Bush's diplomatic efforts as a leader were wanting. Without regard for potential outcomes, his foreign policy actions (as president and as commander in chief) seemed to reflect the overly simple thoughts of a schoolyard bully: "Whom do we hit and when do we hit 'em?" Sadly, he was very much a cowboy diplomat, where his father—in comparison—proved to be the real deal: acting in measured ways and alongside the leaders of other nations. It is not without cause that many in the Middle East view the United States as an evil empire. Since Ronald Reagan sat in the White House, the United States has continued to work toward gaining greater and stronger access to Middle East oil reserves, which has driven much of American foreign policy in the region. Rather than work toward deal-making, though, American activity has been—time and again—bent on undermining existing governments in order to gain access.

If only we had listened to Jimmy Carter, who (in what would be called his malaise speech) cautioned Americans that we needed to find ways to limit our energy dependence on the Middle East. He delivered the accurately titled Crisis of Confidence speech some thirty-five years ago on July 15, 1979. (I do not remember the speech, as I was one month old.)

Noting America's relationship with OPEC (the Organization of Petroleum Exporting Countries: Iran, Iraq, Kuwait, Saudi Arabia, and Venezuela), Carter said, "I am tonight setting the… goal of cutting our dependence on foreign oil by one-half by the end of the next decade." He continued, "To ensure that we meet these targets, I will use my presidential authority to set import quotas… (and) I will forbid the entry into this country of one drop of foreign oil more than these goals allow." Way to go, Mr. President! He went on to detail the need for an energy commission, to research and develop alternative sources of fuel: from coal, oil shale, plant products.

His energy leadership was upended by a Congress that was unwilling to spend what was necessary and unwilling to do potential harm to relationships with the Middle East. Imagine if Americans had taken Carter's message to heart. Perhaps we would be more energy independent (or at the very least we could be dealing more extensively with countries like Canada and Brazil). Perhaps, had we shaken our OPEC dependence, people in the Middle East would not view the United States as a force pushing its weight around, trying to foment discontent and revolution in hopes of seeing friendlier pro-US governments in place.

All this is, of course, speculation. What we do know is that much of the reason for George W. Bush wanting to invade Iraq and oust dictator Saddam Hussein (despite stated claims of a 9/11 terrorist connection that was never concretely made) was the hoped-for potential of having greater unfettered access to Iraq's oil reserves. According to Col. Lawrence Wilkerson, who was Colin Powell's chief of staff from 2002 to '05, "If you know the region as well as I do now, particularly after spending many years in the military doing war planning for the region, it'd be risible for me to say 'it wasn't about oil.' Of course it was about oil."

Bush apologists strongly deny that the United States engaged in war for oil; however, for anyone paying close attention during the campaign season of 2000, the writing was on the wall. In an appearance before a GM production center in October of that year—just one month prior to the election—George W. Bush said, "On the Clinton/Gore watch, Saddam Hussein's Iraq has become a major supplier of oil to America. This means that one of our worst enemies is gaining more and more control over our country's economic future."

One of our worst enemies. Bush was, of course, referring to the man whom the US military had (under the first President Bush) militarily upbraided—literally—in a matter of days. The true level of threat (from a military standpoint) posed to America by the truculent Iraqi dictator was laughable. Economically, in the form of oil, was a different matter. The message was—or should have been—clear: Mr. Bush, if elected, intended to act. And he did.

Of special note, while we dithered in the desert, looking for Iraqi weapons of mass destruction that did not exist, another nation—North Korea—actually was engaged in developing nuclear capability. On October 9, 2006, what was initially thought to be a terrific 4.3 magnitude earthquake turned out to be the detonation of an atomic bomb. While the Bush administration set its eyes on Iraq, it ignored Kim Jong Il's repressive regime.

The destabilization in the Middle East that we have witnessed in the years following Saddam Hussein's removal from power—the lives lost in needless war and in violent revolutions—offers us the painful picture of one leader's bloody legacy: hypocrisy at home and bullets for oil abroad is—and will forever be—President George W. Bush's legacy.

So much for Grant's wish: "Let us have peace."

In 2008, the United States held a presidential election. The hope was "hope." The promise was "change." The following chapters will examine whether or not (or to what extent) we as a nation have successfully turned the corner. Have we done enough to emerge from the shadow of the Bush legacy?

CHAPTER SEVENTEEN

2008/2012

"Rarely in any time does an issue lay bare the secret heart of America itself. Rarely are we met with a challenge—not to our growth or abundance, or our welfare or our security—but rather to the values and the purposes and the meaning of our beloved nation. The issue of equal rights for American negroes is such an issue. And should we defeat every enemy, and should we double our wealth and conquer the stars and *still* be unequal to this issue, then we will have failed as a people and as a nation."

The speaker continued, "Their cause must be our cause, too. Because it's not just negroes, but really it is all of us, who must overcome the crippling legacy of bigotry and injustice. And we shall overcome."

These words, which echoed the popular civil rights anthem of the time, were spoken before a special joint session of Congress on March 15, 1965. They were said not by a charismatic Northern firebrand but by Lyndon Baines Johnson, thirty-sixth president of the United States. For just a moment, imagine: think of hearing those words being delivered with—of all things—a Southern accent! It was a magic moment. This book began with my personal remembrance of Ronald Reagan's speech following the Challenger disaster, with the admission that the final line of that speech tends to put a lump in my throat. The same is true when I hear LBJ's words (I believe it would take a very cynical person, in fact, to have a different reaction).

1965. At a time when lynchings were still carried out in Southern states—where bigotry was law—a man of the South stood (with the power of the Oval Office in his hands) and spoke for those who had for so long suffered with too few powerful men joining their cause. One hundred years after Lincoln's issuance of the emancipation proclamation, LBJ suggested that time was long overdue for America to live up to her promise of equality. He could not know that forty-three years later, a black man would stand in his shoes as president.

The year 2008 was an election year.

After eight years of George W. Bush and Dick Cheney calling the shots (with Mr. Cheney declining to run for the presidency himself), both the Republican and Democratic parties were ready to look to new faces for leadership. The primary season that year would offer voters a crowded cast:

The Democrats were especially ready to reclaim the White House. The candidates were Barack Obama, of Illinois; New York senator (former First Lady) Hillary Clinton; North Carolina senator John Edwards (John Kerry's running mate in 2004); Joe Biden, of Delaware; Governor Bill Richardson, of New Mexico; Evan Bayh, of Indiana; and Chris Dodd, of Connecticut.

The Republican primary stage was no less crowded. The candidates were John McCain, of Arizona; former governor Mitt Romney, of Massachusetts; Governor Mike Huckabee, of Arkansas; Ron Paul, of Texas; "America's mayor" Rudy Giuliani; Fred Thompson, of Tennessee; Tom Tancredo, of Colorado; and Alan Keyes, of Maryland (former US ambassador to ECOSOC—the United Nations Economic and Social Council).

Early in the season, it seemed clear that there were certain "all-stars," and most political pundits thought it was clear that the election would come down to a choice between Hillary Clinton and Rudy Giuliani. Few of the other names could claim the affection or the sizable spotlight—the sheer recognition—that Clinton or Giuliani could command. Giuliani started strong, but his candidacy was undone in self-inflicted fashion when the fault in his stars was highlighted (by Joe Biden). During a Democratic primary debate, Biden said, "There's only three things he [Giuliani] mentions in a sentence: a noun, a verb, and 9/11." Perhaps it was an unfair shot, but the charge (though it must have stung) was largely true: it was rare that the former New York City mayor failed to mention his role during the events of September 11 as illustrating his qualifications for the presidency. He was—is—a good man, but with the political wind taken from his sails, Giuliani withdrew from the race in January of 2008.

Mike Huckabee had early successes, winning the Iowa caucus before winning both the Kansas and Louisiana primaries, but his campaign suffered from too little financial backing. With Giuliani out and Huckabee hoping for third-place finish opportunities in later primaries, the crowd had thinned, leaving McCain and Romney as the favored front-runners. By September, Senator John McCain was—if not the party's overwhelming favorite—in a real sense (after a bruising primary contest) the last man standing and the Republican nominee.

The drama, meanwhile, had been less scorching for the Democrats. Hillary maintained a strong lead in most polls for the better part of the season. But the allure of his magnetic speeches—and the historic possibility, the real potential of electing the first African-American to the presidency—led many in the party to undertake a closer examination of and friendlier look at Barack Obama. Both candidates, in point of fact, were representative of alluring "first" possibilities: a black man and a woman actively looking to be the next president of the United States. An important issue, though—

one that would doggedly haunt Hillary's campaign—was her post-9/11 vote (in October of 2002) in favor of authorizing President George W. Bush's invasion of Iraq. It was this sensitive issue that particularly impressed the author of this book when considering my vote during the primary.

In the end, when the primary dust settled, the 2008 race would be between the Democratic Obama/Biden ticket and the Republican McCain/Palin ticket. Both parties ran campaigns offering a change, taking the country away from the divisive style of leadership as offered by the Bush II administration. Obama was a clear embodiment of change; McCain suggested that his profile as a "maverick" in the senate (who was willing to work with Republicans and Democrats) would make him a different kind of leader, less polarizing than Bush had been. One cannot overstate, then, the impact John McCain's choice for running mate had on the eventual outcome of the election.

Sarah Palin was an unknown, especially in comparison to the men who'd enjoyed (perhaps *enjoyed* isn't the right word) the spotlight during the primary debates. I recall the moment I heard that McCain had announced his choice for a running mate. I was at work. A coworker (the same person I challenged—as described in chapter 6—to name a president who never lied) came over and handed me a piece of paper on which he'd written the last name Palin. He said, "That's it—McCain/Palin." My response was, "Who's that?"

When he gave her complete name, my initial, knee-jerk reaction was that it was a rather transparent, cynical move on McCain's part to attract former Hillary voters. (There is no way to know for certain—other than perhaps interviewing McCain campaign advisors, who would likely never admit it—whether or not this was the case.) What is known is that McCain waited until August (pretty late in the election year) to choose and then to announce his choice for a running mate. There was little time for a comprehensive, in-depth vetting process—a truth that quickly became all too apparent when

Palin's sobering lack of informed thought on the issues was broadcast by television cameras and radio stations. While no one could seriously question John McCain's experience and years of service, the question of Sarah Palin's qualifications to be vice president of the United States created a firestorm.

Her lack of experience was not the only weight threatening to sink the ticket. Sarah Palin belonged more to the far-right wing of the GOP than McCain. Her placement on the Republican ticket was never likely to attract middle-of-the-road (or moderate) voters. McCain advisors surely knew this. The hope was that her presence would be enough to attract and keep hard-core conservative votes (votes that, during the primaries, Mr. McCain had some difficulty in drawing). What history makes clear, however, is that to ignore—or worse, to snub—moderates is not a successful strategy for winning the White House.

The McCain/Palin ticket was, essentially, the physical as well as the symbolic personification of the Republican dilemma.

In his book *What Went Wrong: The Inside Story of the GOP Debacle of 2012*, author Jerome Corsi treated readers to his "autopsy" of Mitt Romney's loss to President Obama. (He actually looked at both the 2008 and 2012 elections to make his argument.) It was—in effect—a recitation of the far right's problem with moderates. Corsi believes that in order to put a Republican back in the White House, the GOP needs to dump so-called centrist candidates like John McCain and Mitt Romney (never mind that, in my lifetime, Republicans who *did* win the White House—Reagan, Bush, and G. W. Bush—were able to appeal to moderate voters). This is something that far-right candidates of Mr. Corsi's preference—Rick Santorum and Sarah Palin, for example—are unable to do.

In both 2008 and 2012, the Republican candidates suffered when they felt sidetracked into answering for the noise created by extremist down-ticket candidates in state elections. Recall, for example, Todd Akin, of Missouri, who was recorded as having offered up what was potentially the most nonsensical comment ever uttered by a candidate for office, saying, "If it's a legitimate rape, the female body has ways to try to shut that whole thing down." (That "whole thing," of course, being an unwanted pregnancy.) Rather than discuss the economic health of the nation—as he certainly would've preferred—Mitt Romney was forced to either agree with or denounce Akin, and was thus drawn into the debate over abortion and the role of government in women's reproductive lives.

Had John McCain not embraced the far-right element with his selection of Sarah Palin as his running mate, the image he had carefully burnished as a consensus-building "maverick" might have fared better. Likewise, had Mitt Romney run as the real Romney (that is to say, as the moderate former governor of a "blue state") rather than bend to the pressure he doubtless felt of having to appear more conservative than he truly was, the outcome might well have been different. The conservative pressure is not a desert mirage or phantasm—it is real. There is no way that Romney could have embraced his actual record vis-à-vis health care, for example. Had he stood firm behind his Massachusetts program, but simply said, "It works, and can be a model *at the state level*" (which would have been an honest approach), the ultraconservatives of the far right (like Mr. Corsi) would have howled. So Romney was forced instead to walk away from his actual record, which was what created so much of his awkward flip-floppy persona.

The damage done, Mr. Corsi, is not when GOP candidates prove to be too "centrist" but that the party has delivered unto itself repeated, self-inflicted losses: having moved—and it has—further into Palin territory and away from the comfort zone where men like John McCain and Willard "Mitt" Romney (not to mention their political godfather Barry Goldwater) stand. It is a middle-of-the-road zone where—like it or not, Mr. Corsi a majority of Americans stand, a point to which 2008 and 2012 results can attest.

It should be no surprise then—with this dynamic of internal combustion at play within the Republican Party (with people like Corsi, Palin, Limbaugh, etc., temperamentally at odds with nominees of John McCain's mien)—that in the election of 2008, Barack Obama won, becoming the nation's forty-fourth president. Party unity (or lack thereof) often looms large as a deciding factor in elections.

Really, it's as if the Republican Party is collectively unaware of its own storied history of fractious disunity. A brief look at the election of 1912 offers a sharp lesson to which the GOP should pay particular attention. In a contest between the liberal and conservative wings for the nomination that year, Republican delegates were split between incumbent president William Howard Taft and former president Theodore Roosevelt. The division (which led to a Roosevelt defection to run as the third party Bull Moose candidate) proved costly, ultimately paving the way for the Democrat, New Jersey governor Woodrow Wilson, to easily win that November. Anyone at all familiar with the history of—and lessons gained from—the year 1912 would have seen John McCain's loss to Barack Obama in 2008 coming a mile away.

Clearly, disjointed matchups (like McCain/Palin) aren't the answer. Unless and until the GOP can put aside the internal differences and coalesce around an overall vision, clearly spelled out for the American public, they will continue to experience small wins in state or local elections and losses at the national level. The ghosts of Taft, TR, and Wilson will continue to haunt the RNC (Republican National Committee).

There were, of course, other elements at play in '08.

One cannot analyze the contest of 2008 without discussing it in terms of race and the history of race relations in the United States, which is one reason for the decision to begin this chapter as I did. When Barack Obama offered "change" as his key promise, he was addressing the idea that his would be a campaign based on a referendum of the Bush II years; however, he was himself—it is impossible to deny, whether he wished to be or not—a symbol of greater change in an historic moment (a "we shall overcome" moment). When Mr. Obama beat out Hillary to become the Democratic Party's nominee, John McCain's aspirations to reach the Oval Office were almost certainly dealt a very large hurdle to overcome. It may not be a fair assessment (I believe it is), but one cannot discount the role that emotion played in '08 voter turnout.

For so many reasons, the election of 2008 proved to be a truly interesting one. I, for one, was glued to the news channels—CNN, MSNBC, FOX—watching the reports through the various primary debates to the nominating conventions.

When Barack Obama took the oath of office on January 20, 2009, with George W. Bush in attendance, I was hopeful. One man was leaving the political stage, the other taking over. The offer—the promise—of "change" sounded good to me. But what would that change mean? Would Obama be the spiritual inheritor of LBJ's liberal vision, or would he chart his own, moderate path? More importantly, would his actual record in office live up to his promise?

The following chapters will be dedicated to the examination of that question.

CHAPTER EIGHTEEN

Keeping Us Safe?

It has been said, time and again, by detractors of President Obama that he has (as commander in chief) failed in his topmost responsibility to keep America safe. This charge has been made—in particular—by those in the conservative media: Sean Hannity, Sarah Palin, and Rush Limbaugh, to name a few. This is a rather amazing suggestion that deserves to be examined, for there can be no stronger or damning accusation made against a sitting president than that he has fallen asleep at the wheel where American safety is concerned. Certainly, if a president *were* to be found derelict in his particular role as the chief protector/defender then—in this writer's mind—he would be open to calls for inquiry for impeachment.

It is difficult, not to say impossible, for anyone to judge *any* presidency until history has had a chance to look at it through the lens of the rearview mirror. It will be difficult to come to a *conclusive* verdict on the Obama presidency in any respect before it is ended. This chapter, therefore, will study President Obama's actions as commander in chief in comparison—whether favorable or not—to the actions of previous administrations. This approach will also afford readers a measure of context with which to consider the failure charge (as described above).

To offer what is perhaps the clearest example of presidential failure—indeed, an example of dereliction of duty insofar as keeping American citizens safe—I might refer readers to the sad figure of James Buchanan, of Pennsylvania, the fifteenth president of the United States. When a man takes the presidential oath of office, he swears to "preserve, protect, and defend" the US Constitution. Mr. Buchanan believed that in condemning the activities of abolitionists in the North (he saw them as domestic terrorists), he was defending the Constitution as it was written. True enough. He failed, however, to fully appreciate that the Constitution in this case—in declaring an entire segment of the American population to be pieces of property—was the problem. He ignored the moral implications of what was happening in the closing years of the 1850s. Of course, it may be said that by the time Buchanan took office, the groundwork for the coming of the Civil War had already been laid. This fails to take into consideration the fact that Buchanan personally intervened in the Supreme Court's Dred Scott decision. which further enflamed North/South tensions. Rather than forestall armed conflict, the president's actions contributed to the hastening of the conflict. The political strength of his friends in the South was foremost in the president's mind; the safety—meanwhile—of the American people on both sides of the moral divide was, for Buchanan, a secondary concern. When South Carolina became the first state to secede from the Union (on December 20, 1860), President Buchanan challenged the legality of secession; in his weakness, however, he claimed he had no constitutional authority to stop it.

The ghosts of Buchanan's failure still haunt the unquiet fields of the Civil War.

Buchanan's example, though, is perhaps too remote for readers to fully appreciate. A more immediate (or modern) example of presidential failure exists in the unfortunate administration of Lyndon B. Johnson, the thirty-sixth president of the United States. President Johnson had great successes in the administration's war on poverty and in wresting concrete change during the civil rights movement;

his foreign policy record, though, will always be a stain on his reputation as a leader. In the summer of 1967, as America waded further into the mire of hostilities in Vietnam, something took place—a tragedy—that the LBJ administration would cover up, lest one of America's "allies" be perceived instead as a bully (so the thinking went). Here is the sad truth:

In June of 1967, the Middle East was swept into the Six-Day War (between Israel and several Arab states). Throughout, the United States maintained neutral status. On June 8, the USS *Liberty* (classified as a technical-research vessel) was in international waters near the northern coast of Egypt, performing signal collection (very likely spy intel, keeping tabs and monitoring the escalating situation), when she was attacked by both Israeli Air Force fighter aircraft and Israeli Navy torpedo boats. Thirty-four *Liberty* crew members were killed, and 171 were wounded. According to Vice Admiral William Martin, the *Liberty* was "a clearly marked United States ship" and "not a participant" in the hostilities when she was attacked. Israeli reports of the incident claimed that the *Liberty* had been mistaken for either (1) an Egyptian ship or (2) a Soviet warship or battle cruiser.

According to intercepted radio communications, at around 2:30 (near the beginning of the attack), two Israeli helicopters were dispatched to the scene in order to verify the identity of the vessel, to determine whether or not the *Liberty* was flying an American flag. This alone would seem to upend Israel's argument that the affair had been a case of mistaken identity. Such reports notwithstanding, the US and Israeli governments conducted investigations into the incident, and both concluded that the attack had been in error.

Survivors maintained that for several hours *before* the attack, they witnessed a number of Israeli flyovers (which, if their accounts are to be trusted, would give every indication that Israeli forces had full opportunity to make visual contact and correctly identify the ship as a "friendly" or "neutral"). This testimony, along with the record of helicopter communications, supports the belief that the attack was deliberate (perhaps to send a message to "keep your distance"?).

In the aftermath of the attack, Israel apologized. In May 1968, the Israeli government paid over $3 million to the families of those killed; in 1969, it paid another $3 million to those wounded; and in 1980, it paid the United States $6 million as a settlement for material damage sustained during the attack. One imagines that Israel would've put up more of a fight in having to pay out such large amounts if the incident had in fact been strictly accidental in nature. To some, there seems to be an odor of guilt that encircles the *Liberty* payments.

The important question must be asked: why would the president of the United States support investigation findings that so clearly contradicted the facts on the ground as witnessed by survivors of the attack?

The sad answer is clear:

President Johnson's primary concern—rather than defend the brave men serving in the US armed forces and call for justice (certainly for recompense) in the occasion of their deaths—was to avoid the potential for an unpleasant international scuffle with Israel over what was clearly an act of unwarranted aggression. He had his hands full as it was (so the thinking went) with the situation in Vietnam. It was a political decision. Americans—the families of those lost in the attack in particular—were told that it was all an accident.

As suggested in previous chapters, another sad example of presidential failure—this one greater in scope (to this writer's mind) than LBJ and the USS *Liberty*—exists in the more immediate history that "we the people" have lived through.

As discussed in chapter 9, President George W. Bush was warned by the CIA on several occasions throughout the fall and summer months of 2001 that the radical group Al Qaida, led by Osama bin Laden, had operatives in the United States and had plans to carry out a deadly attack. No attempts were made to tighten security in the nation's airports, bus terminals, or subway systems. No measures were taken to tighten security at the United Nations building or at the Twin Towers of the World Trade Center (which had previously been the scene of an attack by Al Qaida).

During a White House press conference held March 13, 2002, Mr. Bush was asked a two-part question: (1) if he had any sound intelligence as to Osama bin Laden's whereabouts—in fact, did he know if bin Laden was still alive?—and (2) could he say anything regarding the nature of the threat that bin Laden continued to pose? As discussed in previous chapters, the administration had, at this time, already begun to shift its attention to Saddam Hussein and Iraq. Bush wanted the focus to be on Iraq, not on the elusive mastermind of 9/11, who had yet to be captured. Of course, the president wouldn't be so bold as to dismiss the threat that Osama bin Laden posed, right?

His answer was, "You know, I just don't spend that much time on him, Kelly, to be honest with you." The president went on to discuss how he believed that terror "is bigger than one person." True enough, but bin Laden was the leader of the terrorist organization—leader of the enemy we faced—and as such was an important figure in the struggle. He had orchestrated the 9/11 attack.

The reporter gave President Bush a chance to clarify his position, asking again specifically about Osama bin Laden.

He said, "I truly am not that concerned about him."

One imagines a person who lost a loved one in the rubble of the Twin Towers hearing this. One can only imagine their reaction as military families watched the press conference and heard the commander in chief suggest that the concerted efforts of their sons and daughters in the mountains of Afghanistan was something that he "didn't spend that much time on" and that finding and bringing the leader of Al Qaida to justice was not a concern. Good job, Mr. Bush.

On many different occasions on his television show, Sean Hannity has stated that "President Bush kept us safe." Hannity never has acceded to the fact that Mr. Bush was negligent in the months *leading up to* the attack (a point that was made by former Minnesota governor Jesse Ventura when he was a guest on Mr. Hannity's show—May 18, 2009). Mr. Hannity says—often—that while "President Bush kept us safe," President Barack Obama has not.

On May 2, 2011, President Barack Obama, the man who succeeded George W. Bush (and who has, according to people like Sean Hannity, been negligent in keeping America safe), addressed the nation. He said, "Tonight, I can report to the American people and to the world that the United States has conducted an operation that killed Osama bin Laden." He continued, "It was nearly ten years ago that a bright September day was darkened by the worst attack on the American people in our history. The images of 9/11 are seared into our national memory; hijacked planes cutting through a cloudless September sky; the Twin Towers collapsing to the ground; black smoke billowing up from the Pentagon; the wreckage of Flight 93 in Shanksville, Pennsylvania, where the actions of heroic citizens saved even more heartbreak and destruction."

President Obama was right: these are images that we will never forget.

All because a president of the Unites States—the forty-third—failed to keep us safe.

Where Osama bin Laden is concerned, I will suggest that President Obama's actions stand in far better light than his predecessor's. While Mr. Bush spent eight years promising—in grand, strutting-cowboy fashion—that he would bring those responsible for 9/11 to justice, he failed to do so. In fact, he said that he "truly" was "not that concerned" about bin Laden. It was left to his successor to get the job done.

Killing bin Laden, then, is an Obama win. Where Mr. Hannity and his conservative friends fault the Obama administration must lie elsewhere (and indeed, it does). They see horrible events unfold, like the embassy bombing that took place on September 11, 2012, in Benghazi, Libya, and find that the president was "asleep at the wheel." The argument is made that the president should have done more to protect the Americans who were serving in a hostile atmosphere. Should he—or could he—have done more? Yes. Is this a matter that deserves to be examined in hopes that we act better in the future? Yes. Is it an overreaction to suggest that the president be impeached? Yes.

Should the United States take a closer look at where we have servicemen and women stationed overseas? Yes. Should our elected leaders take steps to rethink our global position, to question whether we should have embassies in certain "hot spots" around the globe (places like Sudan or Libya, for example), where Americans serving their country may be at great risk? Absolutely!

Rather than attack the president, we should pause long enough to ask, "President Obama, given US history in the region, why in the world did we have a US embassy in Libya?" This would be a constructive activity. We as free citizens have every right to ask why if our leaders decide to place our fellow Americans—serving in either a military or civilian capacity—in harm's way. And Mr. Obama needs to be ready with an answer. It is not enough for us to mourn the loss of Ambassador Chris Stevens and the others who died in the Benghazi attack; nor is it enough for us to engage in partisan sniping and faultfinding. "We the people" have to ask the difficult questions, and our president and other elected leaders in the Congress need to answer them.

For the moment, let's set aside Benghazi and examine another, more recent development that has given cause for conservatives to argue that President Obama's actions have endangered—rather than ensure the safety of—Americans. In this particular case, sadly, I am completely inclined to agree.

In May of 2014, an exchange was made, which set the nation into a frenzy. Five Taliban prisoners who were being held at the detention center at Guantanamo Bay were freed in exchange for the release of Sergeant Bowe Bergdahl, a US Army serviceman who had been captured in Afghanistan in June 2009. For some, the action was seen as a humanitarian effort by the administration to secure the release of a long-suffering American; for others, though, the idea that the United States negotiated such a transaction with the enemy was and is (however noble the intent) an unacceptable move—really, an accommodation with terrorists—which will, in the long run, cause more harm than good. The prisoners who were released as part of the exchange were known to have been high-ranking Taliban officials before their capture: the Taliban army chief of staff, the deputy minister of intelligence, an interior minister, and two other senior Taliban officials. In other words, these were not small players in the war on terror.

Following the exchange (even prior to Bergdahl's June 13 return to the United States by way of an army medical center in San Antonio, Texas), it was learned that the circumstances surrounding Bergdahl's disappearance and subsequent capture in 2009 were shady, to say the least. In a *Rolling Stone* article written by Michael Hastings, Bergdahl sent an e-mail to his parents back in the States prior to his capture. According to the article, Bergdahl wrote the following: "Mom and Dad, the future is too good to waste on lies. And life is way too short to care for the damnation of others as well as to spend it helping fools with their ideas that are wrong." He continued, "I have seen their ideas and I am ashamed to even be [A]merican."

Sergeant Bowe Bergdahl (again, according to the *Rolling Stone* article) ended his e-mail with this: "I am sorry for everything. The horror that is [A]merica is disgusting. There are a few more boxes coming to you guys. Feel free to open them, and use them."

The e-mail would seem to indicate that Sgt. Bowe Bergdahl's disappearance from his platoon was in reality a desertion on his part, the act of a man who was disillusioned with his role in the army and was ready to leave it behind. Bad enough the United States negotiated with the enemy. The *Stone* article, taken together with word from several of Bergdahl's fellow soldiers testifying to his disaffection, is rather damning. If these accounts are to be believed, then the president as commander in chief engineered a risky prisoner trade in order to free a man who had—in effect—delivered himself into harm's way (into the hands of the enemy) when he deserted his post. In point of fact, if he *was* a deserter, then he also put his fellow soldiers in harm's way, as they led several missions in search of Bergdahl. Though the Pentagon quickly released a statement saying that it was impossible to confirm, the news network CNN reported that according to some who were involved, at least six soldiers were killed during the search/rescue missions.

The entire Bergdahl affair is a very dark stain on President Obama's record.

Of course, there were plenty of Republicans who were guilty of acting no less foolish. In a Memorial Day message, New Hampshire's senator Kelly Ayotte urged the Department of Defense to continue its efforts to do all it could to find and return Bergdahl; following the prisoner exchange and his release, however, Ayotte (of course) criticized the president. In what I believed to be the most surprising statement made at that time—this, before the exchange—Sen. John McCain, of Arizona (who was himself a prisoner of war during the Vietnam era), initially called the idea for a "swap" a "mistake." (One imagines that his experiences would lead him to encourage any effort to attain the release of an enemy-held prisoner.) Then, the inevitable flip-flop: when asked about the potential for a five-for-one deal in the making, McCain told CNN's Anderson Cooper, "Obviously I would need to know the details, but I would support ways of bringing him home, and if exchange was one of them, I think that would be something I think we should seriously consider."

Republican flip-floppy criticism after the fact notwithstanding, as stated, the affair is indeed a stain on Mr. Obama's record. History, of course, will be the ultimate judge as to whether or not the move proved dangerous. One fervently hopes that the released detainees (the so-called Taliban Five) do not proceed to engage again in future attacks against Americans. If they do, President Obama will have no one else to blame. He will have to wear the responsibility on his shoulders, the blood on his hands.

Now, having examined various administrations and different situations, it will be smart to revisit the question that formed the basis for this chapter: has President Obama failed in his duty to keep America safe? I will have to argue that the answer is a complicated maybe.

It is, for me, far less crystallized than it is in the minds of the president's critics. For such people, Obama is a captain who, standing at the bow of the ship, has led it in a disorganized and ultimately dangerous manner. Especially when taking into consideration how his predecessor, President Bush, handled the ship of state, I must frankly conclude that while President Obama's leadership has been lackluster, he has managed to do far better than his critics suggest. Has his term of office been an unmitigated failure? No. Has it been a rousing success? No. I sadly return, then, to the complicated maybe.

It is this writer's considered opinion that rather than politely listen to those who make the ridiculous claim that George W. Bush kept us safe while Barack Obama has not, we may wish to ignore the likes of Hannity, Palin, and Limbaugh. Theirs are simply voices of *distraction*. We are best served not by the static of such voices but by the clear timbre of our own, when we—as free, thinking Americans—begin to demand of our elected leaders a more vigorous accountability when it comes to national security and the deployment of our armed services.

CHAPTER NINETEEN

War

The Founding Fathers of this nation were wary of seeing too much power vested in the hands of one man. They feared that if he were given unmatched or unchecked powers, a president might succumb to the urge to scratch the itch of corruption and become—essentially—an American dictator. The Fathers fought a revolution in order to shed the shackles of what they saw as foreign tyranny; they hoped the new government structure that they were forming would prevent *itself*—through established checks and balances—from embracing or acting upon the worst aspects of human nature. They translated their fears into specific rules by drafting the US Constitution.

Article I, Section 8, of the Constitution rather unambiguously spells out the various responsibilities of Congress. (Among the specific responsibilities, it mentions the power to lay and collect taxes, to regulate commerce with foreign nations, to establish post offices and post roads, etc.) Importantly, the founders went on in this section to say that the legislative body—the Congress—shall have the power "to declare War, grant Letters of Marque and Reprisal, and make Rules concerning Captures on Land and Water."

Accordingly, when he decided that the United States could no longer safely remain neutral while Europe fought the First World War, President Woodrow Wilson appeared before Congress on April 2, 1917, and made his case for a declaration of war. Four days later,

Congress obliged. On December 8, 1941, Franklin Roosevelt memorably addressed an emergency session of Congress and did just as Wilson had years before: he asked for a declaration of war. Both men followed a constitutionally prescribed path.

In his inaugural address, Ronald Reagan said that "government is not the solution to our problem. Government *is* the problem." In the years following Ronald Reagan's successful rhetorical flourish, Republicans have sincerely adopted the conservative argument against too much concentrated power in the Oval Office. They have fought—hard—to bring influence and power back into the halls of Congress where representatives of the people speak for us. We know that Thomas Jefferson would happily endorse this point of view and course of action.

The educated reader may shrug and say, "Yeah, I already knew that. So?"

In this book's introduction, I briefly described the situation as it then existed in Syria: violent unrest between the Syrian government and her people, with the United States looking on from the sidelines and considering intervention. Thankfully, President Obama (though he was in favor of ordering air strikes) decided against issuing an executive order of action. He called on members of Congress to vote either for or against an authorization for the proposed strikes. Congress held off from taking any immediate action. Fast-forward one year. In recent weeks, Islamic militants—calling themselves ISIS (or the Islamic State)—have gained a foothold not only in Syria but also in neighboring Iraq, pulling Iraq back into the depths of violence. Iraqi forces (having been aided by American military "advisors" for over a decade) proved pitifully ineffectual in defending themselves against the ISIS insurgency. Once again, Iraqi leaders are looking to the West to intercede.

In a recent discussion, a friend suggested that (as examined in the previous chapter) President Obama has not kept America safe.

Specifically, my friend argued that more should be done in an effort to meet the deadly challenge that ISIS forces represent. I do agree with my friend in his thinking that the situation with ISIS in Iraq currently calls for greater US action. In recent days, horrible footage of American journalists being killed—beheaded by ISIS forces—has stirred a terrific discussion across this nation. We do need to act. ISIS is a brutal cancer that the world needs to excise.

My friend went on, however, to lament Mr. Obama's family vacation to Martha's Vineyard and to bemoan images of the president playing golf while "the rest of the world is burning." The picture, my friend argued, was of a president who seemed to provide a callous indifference to the situation rather than true leadership. I offered—for the record—that Congress was also on vacation at the same time, though the president's critics and likeminded news networks seemed not to notice. I then suggested that my friend's anger, while understandable, was a little misplaced. I said that it was Congress's place to "do more," that it was *their* responsibility (rather than the president's) to engage the problem of ISIS.

My friend asked, "Since when?" He recalled the United States' entry into Korea and Vietnam (both of which were undeclared wars, Korea in particular having been called a "police action" by President Harry Truman). He argued that if Mr. Obama were to "pass off" the decision to Congress, then he would be doing so out of a desire not to be holding a political hot potato (as the decision to make war is of great consequence, and those who vote to engage in war—historically—are either celebrated or blamed after the fact).

In response, of course, I referenced Article I, Section 8, of the Constitution. Korea and Vietnam were excellent examples, I told my friend, of what our Founding Fathers wanted *not* to have happen. The hot potato *belongs* in Congress's hands. Speaker of the House John Boehner can bring a vote for action to the floor of the House of

Representatives at any time. Why was my friend's anger directed at the president and not at Mr. Boehner's inaction?

The argument that the president needs to do something more in response to ISIS does not constitutionally "pass the smell test." It is Congress that has not kept America safe. The silence on Capitol Hill has been loud. The voices of our elected representatives need to be heard.

CHAPTER TWENTY

A Question of Energy

A brief look at the United States history vis-à-vis energy has already been undertaken (in discussing President Jimmy Carter's efforts in chapter 16). It is an enticing thing to consider where we as a nation might be today had we paid greater attention to Carter's warnings. Here it will be beneficial to once again quote Richard N. Haass from his book *Foreign Policy Begins at Home: The Case for Putting America's House in Order*. It is an unfortunate, well-known fact that our dependence on foreign oil brings with it substantial geopolitical risks. Mr. Haass says, "The need to import large amounts of oil has… added to the budget deficit, weakened the dollar, and contributed to US economic vulnerability" (p. 130).

"The problem," Haass continues, "is that the United States *consumes* 19 million barrels of oil a day, nearly twice what it *produces*" (p. 130). I have added the italics for emphasis. Obviously, this is an unsustainable situation.

There are positive signs, though: just cause for a more hopeful outlook. In recent years, for example, there have been technological developments in the area of natural gas. It is *necessary*, when formulating a strategic American energy policy for the future, that our leaders include natural gas for two very important reasons: (1) it is a source of energy that, when burned, is less damaging to the environment than oil and (2) the United States is currently the world's largest producer. Development in this area will mean that, rather than rely so heavily upon other nations for our energy needs, America can be more directly responsible for her own economic security (and thus less vulnerable to erratic swings in the global market).

When he took office, President Obama inherited an economic mess. One of his early successes (a promise made during the campaign) was his stated goal of winding down the American commitment of troops in Iraq. The hope was that allowing Iraq to regain its footing and self-composure after a decade of violent disruption will in time lead not only to a less disordered life for Iraqis but also to a measure of more normalized relations between Iraq and other countries. In particular, the potential for a positive relationship between the United States and Iraq—and restored opportunity for trade between the two—would provide obvious energy benefits. Of course, though, this offers a return to (rather than a turning away from) US dependence on Middle East oil.

We need to look elsewhere. We *need* to.

Consider the topic discussed in chapter 19, the ISIS threat and the terrible ongoing events in Iraq and Syria. Herein lies the problem with American intervention/involvement, whether military or economic, in the Middle East. We cannot—*cannot*—allow our future happiness or prosperity to be deeply interwoven with the fortunes of nation-states that have such a disturbing history of violence, of insurrection, and of religious bloodshed. As we have seen in recent weeks, despite our best efforts and wishes, one brushfire often rolls and rages into another. It is not this author's suggestion that the United States cut itself off permanently from the rest of the world; we must, though, consider (in a more careful manner) our strategic goals and the nature and cost of future commitments. We must be especially careful when those goals or commitments involve energy.

On May 4, 2012, the US State Department received an application for a proposed oil pipeline that—if built—would tap into the second-largest petroleum reserve on earth and would run from Canada to an existing pipeline in Nebraska, with an extension that would then run to the Gulf Coast. Critics argue that the pipeline will represent a grave danger to the environment (especially to natural waters). In point of fact, though there are people who oppose the project for reasons having to do with climate control, much of the push-back against the pipeline has less to do with a genuine concern for the environment and more to do with legal arguments over land rights (coming—as it does—from various residents of Nebraska who are unwilling to sell off or lose any portion of land for the project).

There are many people—both Republicans and Democrats—who openly support the Keystone XL proposal. Supporters—I am one—suggest that the pipeline will create jobs (somebody has to build it!) and will benefit the United States through greater access to "friendly" oil. Democratic senator Mary Landrieu, the chairman of the Senate Energy and Natural Resources Committee, is a supporter of the XL pipeline proposal. Her support, given her official position, is especially important. Another voice of support comes from Senator Heidi Heitkamp (D–North Dakota), who, in April of 2014, urged the Obama administration to approve the pipeline. Heitkamp was quoted in the *Washington Post* as saying, "It's absolutely ridiculous that this well-over-five-year-long process is continuing for an undetermined amount of time."

No one wants to knowingly or unnecessarily endanger the environment. But the appeals process has become something of an ongoing tragic comedy, with the administration showing no leadership while it approves delay after delay, with various government agencies assessing groundwater conditions and whether potential dangers to the environment exist. Senator Heitkamp's frustration is indeed well-founded.

As these words are being typed, the Keystone XL proposal is still in limbo. Thus far, the White House has appeared very reluctant to move in either approving or shelving the project. Here is a chance for Mr. Obama—for the president of the United States—to do what his predecessor in the Oval Office (Jimmy Carter) wisely advocated so long ago: lead the country in breaking away from dependence on Middle East oil.

We the people are watching, Mr. President.

CHAPTER TWENTY-ONE

A Bipartisan Prescription?

"The American health-care system is the best in the world." Several friends and coworkers of mine (as well as many people in local, state, and federal government) in recent years have uttered these words when discussing—indeed often arguing over—ObamaCare. As a person who was born with a birth defect (a cleft lip and palate) who has experienced the setback of being denied insurance coverage for certain corrective procedures, I will quickly argue with the above assessment. As it turns out, I am not the only person with a considered, dissenting opinion.

> As a nation, we are doing less than now lies within our power to reduce the impact of disease. Many of our fellow Americans cannot afford to pay the costs of medical care when it is needed, and they are not protected by adequate health insurance. Too frequently the local hospitals, clinics, or nursing homes… either do not exist or are badly out of date… (and) there are critical shortages of the trained personnel

> required to study, prevent, treat, and control disease. (Special message to Congress, January 31, 1955, thirty-fourth US president, Dwight D. Eisenhower, *Republican*)

> Nothing should impede us from doing whatever is necessary to bring the best possible healthcare to those who do not now have it—while improving health care quality for everyone—at the earliest possible time. (Special message to Congress, March 2, 1972, thirty-seventh US president, Richard Nixon, *Republican*)

The Emergency Medical Treatment and Active Labor Act (EMTALA) was passed by Congress in 1986—during Ronald Reagan's second term—and requires hospitals to accept Medicare payments to provide treatment for anyone needing it, regardless of citizenship, legal status, or ability to pay. Reagan, though, was still concerned with the US health-care system.

> Our proposal calls for the Treasury Department and others to find ways of helping families meet these costs... it's too early to predict what will work best, but the important point is that our proposal calls on the government to start working. (Radio address to the nation, February 14, 1987, fortieth US president, Ronald Reagan, *Republican*)

Further along in Mr. Reagan's speech on February 14, 1987, he said, "We will take steps to improve catastrophic illness coverage for all Americans, regardless of age. Under our plan, the Federal and

State governments would work together... to provide insurance for those who could not otherwise obtain insurance."

> Today we spend approximately $1 billion on the medical cost for the uninsured. It is fair to ask all residents to purchase health insurance or have the means to pay for their own care. This personal responsibility principle means that individuals should not expect society to pay for their medical costs if they forego affordable health insurance options. (Signing the Massachusetts Healthcare Reform Act, April 12, 2006, Gov. Mitt Romney, *Republican*)

People who refused coverage—here, the idea of personal responsibility (which has long been a stalwart Republican theme) comes into stark focus—would be fined approximately $1,000 a year, about the same amount they would have paid if they had entered one of the state programs in the first place.

> A future of hope and opportunity requires that all our citizens have affordable and available healthcare. When it comes to healthcare, government has an obligation to care for the elderly, the disabled, and poor children, and we will meet those responsibilities. (State of the Union address, January 23, 2007, forty-third US president, George W. Bush, *Republican*)

Further along in the speech, the resident said, "States that make basic private health insurance available to all their citizens should receive federal funds to help them provide this coverage to the poor and the sick. I have asked the Secretary of Health and Human Services to work with Congress to take existing federal funds and use them to create 'Affordable Choice' grants [which] would give our nation's governors more money and more flexibility to get private health insurance to those most in need."

So, Bush on health care: federal funds for state aid. (But don't call it socialism!)

Senator Ted Kennedy (Democrat) said, "Quality care shouldn't depend on your financial resources, or the type of job you have, or the medical condition you face. Every American should be able to get the same treatment that U.S. senators are entitled to." In other words, health care (like education) should not be just for wealthy sons and daughters with famous last names like Rockefeller, Bush, or Romney.

> This is the cause of my life: new hope, that we will break the old gridlock and guarantee that every American—North, South, East, West, young, old—will have decent quality healthcare as a fundamental right and not a privilege. (Democratic National Convention speech, August 25, 2008, Ted Kennedy)

Uh-oh! A Democrat wants affordable care for all. *Now* it's socialism!

> Six months ago today, a big part of the Affordable Care Act kicked in as healthcare.gov and state insurance marketplaces went live. And millions of Americans finally had the same chance to buy quality, affordable healthcare—and the peace of mind that comes with it—as everybody else.

> Last night, the first open-enrollment period under this law came to an end. Despite several lost weeks out of the gate because of problems with the website, 7.1 million Americans have now signed up for private insurance plans through these marketplaces. (Rose Garden remarks, April 1, 2014, forty-fourth US president, Barack Obama, *Democrat*)

Here, the president acknowledged the rocky start to implementation of his landmark law, the Affordable Care Act (ObamaCare).

Here, however, is where President Obama damaged his program with a wildly self-inflicted wound: "First of all, if you've got health insurance, you like your doctors, you like your plan, you can keep your doctor, you can keep your plan. Nobody is talking about taking that away from you" (spoken to an audience in New Jersey, July 16, 2009). When the Affordable Care Act was passed, the truth came into greater focus. Clearly, there were plans that did not meet the new standards prescribed by the new law. Businesses were made to carry different plans for their employees. Men and women who found they had to switch plans—even carriers—cried foul. The president lied, they said.

Yes, he had.

A great deal of time had been spent developing a workable program, worrying about various ins and outs of a law that would have to be cobbled together by disagreeing political factions—some of whom raged against the very idea of a federal program and who feared the potential (more imagined than real) of government "death panels" and the like—that nobody had addressed the problem of allowing people to keep coverage they liked if that coverage did not measure up to new requirements. Could such language have been written into the law? Absolutely. But the president, in trying to sell the idea to the

American electorate, overreached himself. He promised more than he could deliver. Whether you perceive his comments to be a blatant lie (as many do) or as an exaggeration of hoped-for benefits, the damage in the end was very real. The credibility of statements coming from the Oval Office took a beating. Even the president's supporters had difficulty accepting the fallout.

In politics, it is easy to make promises. It is very good advice, however, to steer clear of making bold pronouncements. For another perfect example, think of the promise made during the 1992 campaign by Vice President George Bush when he became the Republican Party's nominee: "Read my lips, no new taxes." It was a promise that—once in office—he could not keep. Had he lied? Well, not really, no. He had expressed his hope that he would not have to raise taxes. (This, of course, is a much more nuanced message.) But that's not what he said. No nuance, no wiggle room should the need arise, and economic forces require movement on taxes. Just "read my lips." Similarly, Mr. Obama's statement in 2009 regarding his health-care initiative was a bold assertion that left no necessary wiggle room.

What the president should have said was this: "You can keep your insurance so long as the plan you currently have meets the new requirements." But that's not what he said. That's not as flashy, not as easy a sell. In football terms, the president's team had gained several yards on a nice play but had to be called back after a flag was thrown by the American people. It is a shame. Even if—and it is a *big* "if"—history eventually records the Affordable Care Act as a success, the shadow of the lie will hang in the air. The words President Obama so carelessly tossed out without contemplation of possible stipulations will continue to ring in the ears of both his admirers and critics.

Where do we go from here?

From Eisenhower to Obama, the idea that all men—having been created equal, as our Founding Fathers suggested (though didn't always endorse, as many were slaveholders)—should have access to good health care has been something that politicians of both parties have endorsed. As we have seen, presidents and governors alike—Republicans and Democrats—have said much about the inequalities in the American system of health care. All have wanted to see, in their lifetimes, a more just and equitable structure where all Americans (and not just the wealthy) have access to affordable treatment. In fact, the Great Communicator himself, Ronald Reagan, spelled it out rather nicely:

> A catastrophic illness can strike anyone—the young, the old, the middle aged. The single distinguishing characteristic is simply this: whatever form it takes, a catastrophic illness costs money. Lots of it.

True enough. He continued, "All of us have family, friends, or neighbors who have suffered devastating illnesses that threatened their financial security." What then did Reagan recommend in response to this problem? He said, "Our proposal… would take steps to provide… coverage for Americans of all ages" (radio address to the nation, February 14, 1987).

Enter the Tea Party.

"In 2017, I believe a Republican president will repeal ObamaCare in its entirety" (*USA Today* op-ed, October 19, 2014, Senator Ted Cruz, Tea Party). Yeah, never mind the history of Republican presidents—as clearly expressed in their own words—who fought for the idea that all Americans should have equal access to good medical care regardless of background or circumstance. It's those damned bleeding-heart Democrats who're trying to force us all into (gasp!) suffering the evils of greater access and affordability.

> Before Obamacare, there had never been a confirmed case of Ebola in the U.S. (Twitter posting, October 23, 2014, Nick Muzin, senior advisor and deputy chief of staff to Tea Party senator Ted Cruz)

All together now: whaaaaat? Those men and women who charge Democrats with never missing an opportunity to politicize a horrible accident or disaster should take note of the special brand of venom being coughed up by people like Mr. Muzin. With such illogical and hyperpartisan (not to mention clearly mean-spirited) rhetoric surrounding the health-care debate in America, it is no wonder that while we may be better off today than we were, say, forty years ago (to borrow a line from the poet Robert Frost), we still have miles to go before we sleep.

CHAPTER TWENTY-TWO

The Days Ahead

According to James Parton, the first person to attempt a biography of Andrew Jackson—the seventh president of the United States—Jackson was "a patriot and a traitor. He was the greatest of generals, and wholly ignorant of the art of war. He was the most candid of men, and capable of the profoundest dissimulation. He was a democratic autocrat, an urbane savage, an atrocious saint." Parton, in these few words, successfully captured the difficult character of our seventh president. He was, like his country, filled with contradictions. In the prologue of his 2008 book *American Lion*, Jon Meacham had this to say: "Like us and our America, Jackson and his America achieved great things while committing grievous sins" (p. xix).

Both scholars connected the personal character of our seventh president with the young and still-maturing nature of the country he was called to lead. I would argue that we were—in the 1820s and '30s—as we are today in the early years of the twenty-first century: a country (and a people) filled with the potential for both extraordinary goodness and deep injustice. We are an imperfect mix of hero and cynic, of a willingness to expand opportunity and a wish to—in stingy fashion—hoard that opportunity for ourselves. There are those of our number who wish to see a more limited federal government who, too often, condemn our elected leaders in Washington when they do not act quickly or stridently enough (I'm looking at you, Gov. Rick Perry, of Texas).

I will further contend that our imperfect mix, however frustrating it may be, is truly the best that we as Americans can hope for, because it is—in the end—the clearest testament we have to the imperfect humanity that informs the government that "we the people" created so many years ago.

And that is a good thing. Our disagreements—some of which we have been having since Adams and Jefferson were young and dreaming men—are what make us unique among nations. Where other nations have had histories filled with bloody revolution, ours is able to see (though there may be hurt feelings and upset hopes) the peaceful transition of power from one political party to another: without war or bloodshed. For the cynical reader, this fact alone should commend our imperfect system above others. We will continue to disagree. We will continue to have lively, even raucous, debates on issues of great—and sometimes of smaller—importance. And that is a good thing.

We will, as we move forward, continue to elect men and women to represent us to the best of their ability at the highest levels of our government. There will be more saints, more sinners, and—perhaps—there will be a few more like Andrew Jackson, who will occupy a troubled (if distinguished) place in both categories. And, of course, we will continue to differ in our judgments as to who has done right by America and who has done her wrong. As the title of this book suggests, and as the chapters testify (one hopes successfully), I have offered my personal conclusions regarding specific presidents who've held that high office in my lifetime.

It would be arrogant to think or to suggest that every reader will agree with the sentiments I've expressed in the pages of this book, especially at this time in our history, when it seems that our elected leaders cannot agree even on the color of the sky. My hope, in fact, is that there are people who read these pages and who disagree with my conclusions and—rather than dismiss the book as a waste—will engage in a discussion. Ask questions. Make bold assertions. Engage in a dialogue with others who agree or disagree.

Ronald W. Reagan came to the Oval Office in January of 1981, 152 years after Andrew Jackson first took the presidential oath. Both men would leave the country with a "mixed bag" legacy. To borrow Jon Meacham's words, both men—the seventh president of the United States and the fortieth—"achieved great things while committing grievous sins." One cannot examine Reagan's stated hopes, as expressed in his first inaugural address, without also taking the time to consider the record of his accomplishments while in office. The actual record is one that has had—and will continue to have—grave consequences for this nation. Let's for a moment try to draw from the various chapters.

In chapter 18, the matter of "keeping Americans safe" was examined with respect to the charges made against the current president, Barack Obama. When one considers how he needlessly led American military personnel into harm's way in Beirut (as discussed in chapter 4), it must be said that President Reagan failed as commander in chief to protect those 304 brave souls. Additionally, Reagan's later involvement in the Iran-Contra scandal, in which the administration supplied arms to a rogue nation in exchange for the release of hostages, continues to cast a long and haunting shadow, as evidenced by the troubling Bergdahl affair (President Obama's Taliban prisoner exchange discussed in chapter 18). One must eventually come to the considered belief that the role Ronald Reagan played in our history—the "role of a lifetime" as it has been described by some historians—was a damaging one to American honor, credibility, and… yes… American safety.

The damage done was multiplied tenfold during the two stormy terms of the George W. Bush presidency. For those who today rage—with just cause (for theirs is an honest point of view)—against the expanding powers of an overly involved federal bureaucracy, it is an unavoidable truth that their anger must rest at the feet of the forty-third president. The warrantless wiretapping and other unsavory acts carried out by intelligence officials—all in the name of greater protection—began in the weeks and months following the September 11 attacks. Such activity had no stronger defender than the man then living at 1600 Pennsylvania Avenue (and of course, his VP Dick Cheney). While Mr. Obama must answer for *continuing* the secret practices, he cannot be made to take full responsibility (as repeatedly suggested by Republicans with poor memories) for *implementing* them.

To reexamine Mr. Bush's role in the Middle East, I feel, would be to needlessly kick at a dead horse. I have provided several chapters relating to W's foreign policy initiatives. To appreciate the disastrous Bush II legacy, one has simply to turn on any of the 24-7 news networks—CNN, FOX, MSNBC—and can be treated to awful images being reported from Iraq (where ISIS, as discussed in chapter 19, is terrorizing humanity on a heart-breaking level). While no one will ever rightfully call Saddam Hussein a good man, this much can be said: that under his iron-fisted watch, warring factions and such groups as ISIS were kept from gaining a true foothold in the region. Hussein's removal from power has created the kind of power vacuum that prescient men (like Brent Scowcroft, as we have seen in chapter 12) hoped to avoid.

If there are saints and sinners in United States history, then I must maintain that George W. Bush is one of our sinners.

The administration of our forty-fourth president, Barack Obama, is still in the making. His first four-year term ended, and he is now (as this page is being written) in the second year of his second term. It is, therefore, too soon to write the definitive account of his time in office. What scholars and history buffs *can* do is look at what has happened thus far in the broader context. Has President Obama successfully given his fellow Americans the "change" that was promised—time and again—during the 2008 campaign?

I would argue that—no—he has not.

There are reasons, of course (not the least of which has been the existence of a formidable opposition in the Republican-led House of Representatives). In 2010, when Republicans gained control of the House, Mitch McConnell (R-KY) was quoted as saying, "Our top political priority over the next two years should be to deny President Obama a second term." Not job creation. Not immigration reform. The top priority for Republicans was to erect a brick wall over which the president of the United States could not climb. Yikes.

I was told in a conversation just the other day that Mr. Obama has failed to constructively compromise with leaders of the opposition party. My reaction was, "How is a person supposed to find compromise when there is an atmosphere—as exists in Washington today—of such a heated level of obstruction and resistance?" When the person sitting across from you at the table boldly announces that he has made your failure his priority, compromise becomes a fanciful notion. Through much of this book I did challenge Ronald Reagan; however, I must take a moment to commend his ability to deal with Democrats—Speaker of the House Tip O'Neill in particular—as being rather admirable. Mitch McConnell (and likeminded friends) can stand to learn a thing or two from the Gipper.

There are readers who may question the choice I made in not fleshing out a chapter offering deeper analysis of the Obama presidency vis-à-vis the fight over health care. Certainly, passage of the Affordable Care Act (ACA, or what has become known as ObamaCare) was a large milestone for the administration. Indeed, whole books can be written on the subject. Why address it in the limited manner as was done in chapter 21? An argument can be made, and I will so argue, that some of my personal thoughts regarding aspects of health care were provided in chapters 14 and 15.

I believe that one of our two great political parties has, over time and to our detriment, embraced religious argument in political dialogue and legislation. This "discoloration of ideology" has had important consequences for each of us as individual Americans. Republicans, who decry an intrusive government, have fought hard to see ObamaCare either repealed or reformed (going so far as to endure a sixteen-day government shutdown in 2013 rather than support a budget that upheld the ACA); meanwhile, they approve measures that intervene in the most sensitive and private decisions (like abortion) that should be left between a person and her doctor. This hypocritical tendency has damaged the GOP's credibility in many moderate (or purple) states.

And, of course, the fight over ObamaCare is ongoing. A chapter that deals (however effectively) with that continuing fight will—necessarily—end very abruptly. Perhaps chapter 21 does this. As previously stated, though, it is too early to write the current administration's closing chapters. We will have to wait and see.

As stated in the introduction to this book, it is time for both political parties to take certain steps toward becoming more truly representative of the people. Through both a lack of energy and focus (Democrats) and a determined effort to court religious voters (Republicans), our government has grown unwieldy. Government has spiraled "beyond the consent of the governed." It is time to reverse this trend. People want government to work, not for politicians to blindly fight one another with no resolution in sight.

In the days ahead, it is fervently hoped that Americans will (1) take the time to know some of their shared history and (2) engage in political discussions. It is too easy to dismiss an opposing argument if one does not have the relevant historical evidence to back up his own assertions. It is also—I believe—folly to assume that some discussions are too sensitive to engage in. Disagreement is not un-American; in fact, it is *particularly* American. I struggled with the dilemma of how I could best end this final chapter, and I have decided to allow Thomas Jefferson—Founding Father and third president of the United States—to have the honors: "We are all Republicans, we are all Federalists."

A Note on Source Attribution

The following source materials were essential to my understanding of the various historical times discussed in the chapters of this book. Some, but not all, of the books listed were directly referenced and, in each case, were cited accordingly. Those not directly referenced were works that I read in the past, which provided me with an interest in the subject matter and in fleshing out my own opinions. Along with written materials, I found video recordings of enduring value and have listed (and cited) them as well. I owe a terrific debt to the many authors, historians, archivists, and video producers whose work allowed me to build a framework of knowledge that led to this book.

Cannon, Lou. *President Reagan: The Role of a Lifetime*. First trade paper ed. New York: PublicAffairs, a Member of the Perseus Books Group, 2000.

Cheney, Dick. *In My Time*. Paperback ed. New York: Threshold Editions, a division of Simon & Schuster Inc., 2011.

Cockburn, Andrew. *Rumsfeld: His Rise, Fall, and Catastrophic Legacy*. New York: Scribner, a division of Simon & Schuster Inc., 2007.

Deaver, Michael K. *A Different Drummer: My Thirty Years with Ronald Reagan*. Hardcover, 1st ed. New York: HarperCollins Publishers, 2001.

Goldwater, Barry. *The Conscience of a Conservative*. New York: MJF Books (published in arrangement with Regnery Gateway Inc.), 1990.

Greenhouse, Linda. *Becoming Justice Blackmun*. Paperback ed. New York: Times Books (Henry Holt and Company), 2006.

Greenwald, Glenn. *A Tragic Legacy: How a Good vs. Evil Mentality Destroyed the Bush Presidency*. New York: Three Rivers Press (an imprint of the Crown Publishing Group), a division of Random House Inc., 2007.

Haass, Richard N. *Foreign Policy Begins at Home*. Paperback ed. New York: Basic Books, a member of the Perseus Books Group, 2014.

Isikoff, Michael, and David Corn. *Hubris: The Inside Story of Spin, Scandal, and the Selling of the Iraq War*. New York: Three Rivers Press (an imprint of the Crown Publishing Group), a division of Random House Inc., 2006, 2007.

Maddow, Rachel. *Drift: The Unmooring of American Military Power*. New York: Broadway Paperbacks, a division of Random House Inc., 2012.

McCartin, Joseph A. *Collision Course*. Paperback ed. New York: Oxford University Press Inc., 2011.

Middendorf, J. William, II. *A Glorious Disaster: Barry Goldwater's Presidential Campaign and the Origins of the Conservative Movement*. New York: Basic Books, a member of the Perseus Books Group, 2006.

Meacham, Jon. *American Lion: Andrew Jackson in the White House*. Trade Paperback ed. New York: Random House, 2008.

Naftali, Timothy. *George H. W. Bush*. New York: Times Books (Henry Holt and Company), 2007.

Pious, Richard M. *Why Presidents Fail*. Maryland: Rowan & Littlefield Publishers Inc., 2008.

Reagan, Michael. *The New Reagan Revolution*. New York: Thomas Dunne Books (an imprint of St. Martin's Press), 2010.

Reagan, Ronald W. *Speaking My Mind: Selected Speeches*. Paperback ed. New York: Simon & Schuster Paperbacks, 2004.

Reeves, Richard. *President Reagan: The Triumph of Imagination*. New York: Simon & Schuster Paperbacks, 2006.

Zelizer, Julian E. *Jimmy Carter*. New York: Times Books (Henry Holt and Company), 2010.

Essential Video Sources

"Bush's War." *Frontline.* Michael Kirk (director), David Fanning (executive producer). Kirk Documentary Group LTD. PBS Home Video. WGBH Educational Foundation, 2008.

"George H. W. Bush." *American Experience.* Sharon Grimberg (senior producer), Austin Hoyt (director/producer), Callie Taintor Wiser (producer). PBS Home Video. WGBH Educational Foundation, 2008.

"Jimmy Carter." *American Experience.* Sharon Grimberg (series producer), Adriana Bosch (writer/producer/director), David Condon (co-producer). PBS Home Video. WGBH Educational Foundation, 2002.

"LBJ." *American Experience.* Sharon Grimberg (series producer), David Grubin (writer/producer), Chana Gazit (senior producer), David McCullough (narrator). PBS Home Video. North Texas Public Broadcasting Inc., 1991.

"Mr. Conservative: Goldwater on Goldwater." *HBO Documentary Films.* CC Goldwater (executive producer), Judith Aley (archivist), Nancy Abraham (supervising producer), Julie Anderson (director). Sweet Pea Films LLC, 2006.

"Reagan." History Channel program. Matthew Ginsburg (writer/director), Robert Palumbo (producer), Russ McCarroll and David McKillop (executive producers for History). A&E Television Networks LLC, 2011.

"Reagan." *American Experience.* Mark Samels (senior producer), Adriana Bosch (writer/producer, part 1), Austin Hoyt (writer/producer, part 2). WGBH Educational Foundation, 1998. PBS Distribution, 2009.

About the Author

Craig M. Farnham was born in Bridgeport, CT in June of 1979. He attended the University of CT as a literature major and is the author of one previous book: a collection of poems published in 2004 entitled "Stranger Through the City." For some twenty years, he has dedicated much of his free time to writing (always with Bob Dylan or CCR playing in the background) and to the study of American political history. He is a writer, though he makes his living otherwise: as an electrical assembler at Sikorsky Aircraft in Stratford, CT. He lives in Waterbury, CT.

CPSIA information can be obtained
at www.ICGtesting.com
Printed in the USA
FSOW02n2147141016
26168FS